To Be a Presbyterian

LOUIS B. WEEKS

John Knox Press
ATLANTA

Unless otherwise indicated Scripture quotations are from the Revised Standard Version of the Holy Bible, copyright, 1946, 1952 and © 1971, 1973 by the Division of Christian Education, National Council of the Churches of Christ in the U.S.A. and used by permission.

Quotations from the *Book of Order*, 1983–85 are used by permission from the Interim Co-Stated Clerks of the General Assembly of the Presbyterian Church (U.S.A.).

Grateful acknowledgement is made to the members and ministers of Anchorage Presbyterian Church whose names and words appear in this study.

Library of Congress Cataloging in Publication Data

Weeks, Louis, 1941–
  To be a Presbyterian.

  Includes bibliographical references.
  1. Presbyterian Church. I. title.
BX9175.2.W43 1983   285'.1   83-48145
ISBN 0-8042-1880-3

© copyright John Knox Press 1983
10 9 8 7 6 5 4 3 2
Printed in the United States of America
John Knox Press
Atlanta, Georgia 30365

For
Carolyn, Lou, and Sid,
who also contribute to
the life of the church,
and to the vitality of
Anchorage Presbyterian

Contents

Introduction

"What does it mean to be a Presbyterian?" Peggy Cunningham asked a straight question. I tried to give a direct answer. I told her and the other members of the Issues Class we share about some of the special theology of Reformed churches and about Presbyterian styles of government. Actually, Peggy had a very good understanding of what Presbyterians believe; but she had not grown up as one, and she lacked confidence in her knowledge. After class, she and her husband Bill both said they surely would appreciate a study to teach more about the church they had joined in adulthood.

"My cousins and uncles were Buddhists as I grew up," Peggy explained. "I joined a Congregationalist church because they kept up a dialogue with the other living religions. After I moved from Honolulu, Hawaii, to the U.S. mainland, we belonged to several different denominations. We joined here because this church tries to help those in need, and the worship suits our faith."

The Faith Pilgrimage

Many of us Presbyterians, as Peggy Cunningham, did not grow up in Christian families. Many more of us, perhaps a majority of Presbyterians in America today, have belonged to other Christian denominations. We have become Presbyterians for a whole range of reasons. We liked the minister. Good friends belonged to a local Presbyterian church. Someone from the church helped us in times of crisis. We want to help other people, and we find the local church an effective place to serve. We also find many like-minded people, frequently ignorant about the specific history and nature of the Presbyterian Church, but eager to be good Christians all the same.

As I teach and preach in different congregations across the country, I like to ask about the religious pilgrimage of Presbyterians. One young man in a church in Duluth, Minnesota, still holds the record for "frankness." "I just joined this church," he told me, "because my wife had begun coming here. I want our kids to be raised with good values." He wondered aloud if some book would help explain the beliefs of Presbyterians. I suggested the Bible, and we laughed together. Now he personally may have been excessively modest about his own faith, but many Presbyterians share his expressed reasons for being in the church.

One of the questions I like to ask in a Presbyterian group has to do with this pilgrimage. "Will you tell us about your religious background?" The results are usually fascinating, and most of the time someone will thank me for asking. One person said, "Presbyterians seem to assume all of us have always been Presbyterian." As the members of most groups tell about their personal history, most will confess (and many will brag!): "I grew up Methodist"; "My parents were Catholic"; "Well, I was born again in the Assemblies of God, then I became a Baptist"; "We were Lutheran, but this Presbyterian church was in the community and closest in style to ours back home."

No wonder it is difficult in most congregations, indeed in many sessions, to assume that knowledge of the Reformed tradition is a shared perspective. In a seminar in Muskingum Valley Presbytery in Ohio, an older minister said with humor and some sadness, "I kept trying to preach Calvinism; and after several years I guess somebody got up the courage to say after worship one day 'Who was this man Calvin, anyhow?'" Another minister chimed in that she discovered many people could not follow her when she assumed knowledge of words like "regeneration" and "sanctification."

It should be noted quickly that Presbyterians did not enjoy "good old days" when everyone knew the tradition and lived it. Actually, there may be more reading of the Bible today than ever before. Many Presbyterian seminaries now for the first time in American history require a reading of *The Institutes of the Christian Religion*, the work by Calvin on which most Reformed theology has been based. A few generations ago, Presbyterian seminarians came from Presbyterian families, and they had been forced to learn one interpretation of Calvinism from the *Westminster Standards*, the major curriculum for Christian education in the churches. In America this meant a rather tightly-constructed worldview was a part of the experience of most Presbyterians; and those who could read the Bible centered upon it.

Today many more different kinds of reading and viewing are available for people. Newspapers and television present worldviews that differ greatly from traditional Presbyterian perspectives. The ecumenical movement also helps bring many varieties of Christian belief to bear on the lives of Presbyterians. Works of fiction, movies of many kinds, results of the social and natural sciences, all bombard our senses with important and worthwhile learnings. The very learning that can help in mutual understanding and the gaining of wisdom can also interfere with the transmission of tradition.

Questions for the Study

In this context, not necessarily better or worse than previous Presbyterian situations, people and leaders in the churches are asking with increasing frequency for an honest and useful presentation of basic beliefs. What do people "have to believe" to be Presbyterians? What are the beliefs necessary in order to be a leader in the church, a ruling elder or a minister? What other beliefs are important but not essential in Reformed communions?

In perhaps even more profound ways, people ask about the meaning of Presbyterian beliefs for Christian living. What beliefs and practices do Presbyterians share with all the rest of Christ's body? How does the theology of the church relate to salvation of people? What do the authority of the Bible and the tradition affirmed mean in everyday, human situations? How do beliefs about God, Jesus Christ, the Spirit, and the church affect values and decision making?

These questions, and others like these, are phrased in terms of comparison: "What is the difference between Baptists and Presbyterians on the Lord's Supper?" Sometimes they are not phrased at all, merely implied: "I think this congregation should have more meetings and decide the important things for the church by majority votes!"

Most Presbyterians seem honestly to want to be faithful in their allegiance to Jesus Christ and their commitment to the church. They seek to know the implications of their Presbyterian affiliation.

This study is written in response to questions and statements such as these by people in local churches. I write for folk who did not grow up learning the *Children's Catechism*, those who have not yet made their way through the *Westminster Standards* or Calvin's *Institutes*, and those who have not yet fully studied the other creeds that form part of the Reformed tradition in the United States of America. The work is meant primarily for adults; but creative teachers can use it easily with younger, confirmation-age Christians.

I believe strongly, and I want to share my belief, that Presbyterians have had a special presence in America and we have particular contributions to make in our society. I grant the same convictions from Catholics, Lutherans, Baptists, Greek Orthodox, and others. As a Presbyterian, I am deeply engaged in a tradition that offers me food and drink both nourishing and appetizing. I am delighted whenever I have the opportunity to share this diet with other people. By the same token, I know and enjoy the fact that every Christian does not exist on the Reformed diet. I eagerly hear and worship with those of other traditions.

The wider faith, beyond and beneath our particular faiths, does remain primary. No study of Presbyterianism can ignore the vast areas of common faith and action. In this age of denominational mobility and ecumenical cooperation, we just assume the sharing of the Christian responsibility to "feed the hungry, clothe the naked, care for the needy." We assume also the shared call to "make disciples of all nations." We hear together the promises of Jesus, and we together pray for God's kingdom to come "on earth, as it is in heaven."

By the same token, I see real problems for people who do not make a portion of the Christian faith their tradition. After all, the heritage includes all the past history of humankind, for Christians, all of church history. Among the mixed elements of this heritage each of us claims a part of tradition, actively informing life and faith. In the United States today, some of us are tempted simply not to claim a particular tradition. The whole heritage merely washes over us. We define ourselves vaguely as "Protestant Christians." I think the better definition might be "Undifferentiated Religious." How much better it would be if people who want to be Christian maintained the health and vitality of a particular tradition.

Personally, I find the Reformed tradition a good place "on which to stand." From its perspective other traditions make sense, and I can see merits in each. Thus the study is written from an ecumenical, but also especially from a Reformed point of view. When tragedy has struck close to me, Presbyterian tradition has offered an avenue of real Christian solace. When world events seem out of hand, or when I am prone to doubt God's care or justice, Reformed faith has stood me in good stead. I see its promise for the believer, for the church universal, and for the whole creation. But always its promise comes as a portion of the full Christian faith that supersedes all special Christian traditions.

Basic Outline

The study begins with the very basic beliefs of Presbyterians— those required for membership in the denomination. Presbyterians are Christians first and last. We believe with Simon renamed Peter that Jesus is "the Christ, the Son of the living God" (Matt. 16:16). We trust God, the Creator and provider of all good things. We believe with the Apostle Paul that "God was in Christ, reconciling the world to himself" (2 Cor. 5:19). And we believe Christ's Spirit, the Holy Spirit, is sustaining us all in Christian life, giving us God's gifts through all our lives. The first four chapters tell about these basic beliefs and the ways in which we have received them.

Chapters 5 through 8 describe the ways in which Presbyterians have focused in particular fashion on their religious life. Traditional piety and ethics have been hallmarks of Reformed life, involving the whole person in service to God and to neighbors. "What does the LORD require of you," the prophet Micah asked, "but to do justice, and to love kindness, and to walk humbly with your God?"

(Mic. 6:8). At the same time, Presbyterians have celebrated the sacraments of the Lord's Supper and baptism as a portion of the Christian response to God's work in Christ. Again, the understanding of the work of these sacraments has retained a distinctive flavor in Presbyterian churches.

The final four chapters tell some things about citizenship in the Reformed church family. What does it mean to participate responsibly in the church itself? What of the society of which the Christian is part? How are Presbyterians members of the communion of the saints?

The divisions in this study, although rather traditional, are nevertheless arbitrary. The main characteristic of classical Reformed faith has been that everything fits together in a whole. The Christian faith, the Reformed perspective on it, does not collect a group of different ideas and experiences and try to fit them together. On the contrary, Presbyterians celebrate the creative and purposeful work of God, as we have come to know it in Christ Jesus, by the grace of the Spirit. We in turn live creatively and purposefully in all we are and all we do, both in church and in work, in play and in prayer. In the words of Paul, "We know that in everything God works for good with those who love him, who are called according to his purpose" (Rom. 8:28). At several points this important theme will recur, for in our complex and often fragmented world, demonic forces pull us away from this center in God's wholeness.

One final introductory note—the illustrations in this book will come from actual people and churches. Most of the examples, as the one in the beginning, come from the congregation in which my family and I participate. My choice of real people and historical events is partly from habit, because I teach church history. But I like to think it comes mainly from Reformed theology. In our affirmation of the "priesthood of believers" we say in effect that we intercede with one another before God. We teach each other about God's care and forgiveness, about living in the world and anticipating God's kingdom. We all learn through the lives and work of others, and I seek to turn our attention to that process wherever possible.

My choice of illustrations also relates to the ways in which this study will be most useful for groups, classes, and individuals. Please try to think of your situation as you read and discuss the various topics. As I mention Peggy Cunningham, who grew up in Hawaii, you may think of other persons of quite different backgrounds. As I talk about ministers in our local congregation, I hope you will make a definite translation into your own circumstances. As I give examples about the decisions others make and the prayers they pray, I hope you will think about your own. The more these various subjects can be related to your own Christian faith and life, the more helpful the study will be.

1

To Be a Christian

"Sister Carmelita, welcome!" Wayne Perkey, who leads the Issues Class in our church school, introduced the nun who heads a Neighborhood Visitor program in which we share. "We're glad you're here," he said. "You help remind us that we Presbyterians are just one part of the whole body of Christ."

We Presbyterians need to remember how wide and diverse the Christian church really is. We affirm our membership in the one, holy catholic church—the church universal. Our Christian community includes people throughout the whole world whose faith sometimes seems quite different from our own. Wayne Perkey, a member of the session at our church, knows from experience how varied the church can be even in our middle-sized city. When he serves as emcee each year for a Crusade for Children, sponsored by the radio and television stations he works for, all kinds of congregations and church groups give money and time to help. Sister Carmelita knows too how varied and different the churches can be. She belongs to a Roman Catholic religious order, and she is responsible for helping the poor. The Neighborhood Visitor program gives emergency food and money for rent and utilities, and pastors refer people there for service.

Catholic, Baptist, Christian (Disciples of Christ), Lutheran, Episcopal, Methodist, and Presbyterian churches cooperate. All of us Protestants should know about that diversity, yet we all share the catholic heritage. That word "catholic" at one level simply means "universal." All Christians call Jesus the Christ.

A Look at the Family Tree

As Jesus of Nazareth walked, taught, healed people, called disciples, lived, died, and "rose again from the dead," he came to be received by believers as "the Christ, the Son of the Living God." People who came to believe that creed, that "Jesus (is the) Christ," moved from Judaism into a new religious identity related to it. In Antioch (Acts 11:26) they were first called "Christians." Early in their forming process, and following the gospel they had heard and believed, Christians decided that new members of the community did not first have to become Jews, nor did they have to *do* anything else in order to belong. All the *doing* of God's will had been done in Christ. God's promises revealed that truth also. Jesus the Christ called people to faith. From life in the Spirit flowed new ways of living.

The Acts of the Apostles tells of a time when the whole Christian church was one. "Now the company of those who believed were of one heart and soul" (Acts 4:32). One major episode in Acts follows that conference in Jerusalem, when diverse opinions threatened to split the church. There Paul, Barnabas, and Peter prevailed to lead the church in settling its argument on requirements for membership. The church, according to that narrative, came to one accord and remained undivided (Acts 15:25).

Quickly, however, the religious organization of people who followed Jesus Christ began to develop in different ways. Where persecution occurred, some Christians moved underground and worshiped secretly. Others became bold missionaries and sought to convert their persecutors. Some looked forward to God's kingdom dawning, and they saw martyrdom as a step toward that end. Still others, in areas of less overt hostility, tried to explain their new faith in the language of other cultures and philosophies.

The Christian church divided into many parts. Major splits occurred as leaders considered the nature of the Christ they sought to follow. Every council affirmed an "orthodox" (right opinion) position, and every council cut off other avenues of talking and believing in Christ. Through almost all Christian history, different wings of the church have pronounced "anathema" (curse) on "heresies" (choices) and frequently punished heretics. In our own day, many Christians still jealously guard their own brand of faith as though it were the only one. Reformed Christians historically have recognized that other communions also bore a portion of God's truth for the world. Frequently, though, when Presbyterians have spoken of "the church," they have meant just their own little congregation or denomination. We do well to remind ourselves that we Presbyterians are just one branch on the Western limb of the Christian family tree. To be specific, Christians in Presbyterian churches are in the Western, Reformed, evangelical tradition. We follow many patterns of the Roman Catholic Church. We hail from the Reformed, or middle tradition in Protestantism. We consider the gospel at the center of our faith. A further word about each of these terms may be helpful.

The Western Church grew from the Latin-speaking Christian communities, with Rome becoming their natural center over a period of time. The Roman Church came to be distinguished from the Eastern, Greek-speaking communities of Christians not only because of language differences, but because the Western Church recognized the Roman bishop as more powerful than the rest. The Eastern, or Orthodox, Church moved gradually to recognize the honorary primacy of the bishop of Constantinople; but each of the self-governing churches in Alexandria, Jerusalem, Antioch, or more recently in Russia, Bulgaria, etc., possesses great independence from the rest. Another group of "Orthodox" churches separated even further from the Eastern and Western branches when disagreements occurred about the nature of the Trinity. Those communions, such as the Syrian and Armenian, are Christian also. But the Presbyterian communions grew from the Western, or Roman Catholic Church, that separated from the Eastern Orthodox Church finally in 1054.

The Western Church has generally called itself "Catholic." During the Middle Ages, leaders in the Western, Catholic Church tended to grant increasing power to the Pope, the Bishop of Rome, though many among them argued in behalf of ecumenical councils having the greater power. Proponents of papal power cited the words of Jesus: "you are Peter, and on this rock I will build my church" (Matt. 16:18). Simon Peter received the special authority from Christ to "bind and loose" on earth according to this interpretation and Peter became the first bishop of Rome. In the Western, Catholic Church (as in the Eastern Orthodox Church), believers were related to God and to the rest of the faithful primarily through the sacraments.

Within the Western, Catholic Church critics such as John Wycliffe in England and John Huss in Bohemia (Czechoslovakia) argued that the people were being ignored. Church leaders concentrated on gaining lands and political power under the banner of Rome, while they did not even let common people share in the elements of the mass. Why, people could not even understand the Latin of the priests or read the Bible in their own languages! Such criticisms went unheeded by papal heads of the church and the Reformation of the sixteenth century split the Western Christian community. In more recent times, Presbyterians have often forgotten that all of us, Catholic and Protestant, belong to this Western branch of Christianity. Sister Carmelita, the Roman Catholic nun who shares our neighborhood ministry, also shares our family heritage in Western Christianity.

Reformation and Reformed

When Martin Luther in Germany and Ulrich Zwingli in Switzerland led protests against the Catholic Church to which they belonged, various distinct branches of Western Christianity came to have particular identity. At the same time, in the early sixteenth century, Henry VIII, King of England, led a political split from Rome that resulted in a church division. As the Bible became available in various languages for people to read for themselves, more radical interpretations by some resulted in still another, "Anabaptist," movement among Western Christians. From Luther came the Lutheran churches, usually in Europe associated with political governments. From Henry VIII and his successors on the British throne came the Church of England and its offspring in various colonies—one of which became eventually the Episcopal Church in the U.S.A. The Methodist churches also came from Anglican beginnings. From the Anabaptists, came Mennonites, Amish, Hutterites, and some influence for what have become Baptist churches in America. Far more important in starting Baptist communions, and indispensible for what are today Presbyterians, were the Reformed churches claiming Zwingli as one early leader.

Reformed leaders such as Zwingli, John Calvin, John Knox, Martin Bucer, and others, tried to purify the church morally and to restore it to its early patterns of worship and work. They, together with other Protestants, considered faith more important than sacramental ties. Luther had pointed to the promise of Paul, in the letter to the Romans, that "He who through faith is righteous shall live" (Rom. 1:17). Paul had been quoting Habakkuk (2:4); and Luther saw in all the prophets, law, and gospel this theme as the core of the Bible's proclamation. If the Bible offered a true revelation of God's truth for people, then it should be followed where possible. Though Protestants held many beliefs in common, the Reformed wing came to distinguish itself in several areas of biblical interpretation and church government.

Its name, "Reformed," evidently appeared first in France. By the end of the sixteenth century it was in general use throughout Europe.

The Reformed family of churches included some who focused upon the passage in which Jesus promised to be "where two or three are gathered in my name" (Matt. 18:20). Some of these Reformed Christians tried to separate themselves from the government of the state in which they lived. Others tried to have their definition of the church become the official one for people in the realm. Both of these kinds of Reformed Christians belonged to the "Congregationalist" wing of the family.

Presbyterians, on the other hand, sought to include all baptized Christians within the church. Presbyterians paid close attention to the prayer of Jesus that "they may be one," even as he was one with God (John 17:11). Presbyterians advocated representative church government, and they saw the whole church as less prone to err than any particular Christian on his or her own. Presbyterian-type churches became the official religion in Scotland and in portions of the European continent.

As the two wings among Reformed communions grew to distinguish themselves, they continued to cooperate closely in most lands. Their Reformed theology differed little in other respects. John Calvin, whose *Institutes of the Christian Religion* (1536–1559) became a classic statement for Reformed Christians, could be claimed by both the Congregationalists and the Presbyterians.

While this introductory work emphasizes distinctive characteristics of the Reformed churches, it is important to remember that Protestants all share more in doctrine and perspective than they may diverge. Since the Second Vatican Council, it seems to me that Catholics also greatly resemble Protestants in theology and worldview. In fact, the substance of the ecumenical movement affirms today that all together constitute the body of Christ, all are truly Christians.

Christians All

Followers of Jesus Christ have always been called Christians, at least ever since those believers in Antioch received that name. The label has stuck with the whole body of believers throughout history, and it has remained the most inclusive designation for the whole church. To be a Christian meant from the very beginning that a person belonged to a community of faith. Christianity began and remains for the most part a corporate religion.

Presbyterians, and many other branches of the Christian church, have tried to continue the tradition of that first community described in the Acts of the Apostles. Part of the life of faith involved listening to the disciples, fellowship, the breaking of bread, and prayers (Acts 2:42). Another part consisted in the sharing of all they had, both with others in the household of faith and with those who were needy (Acts 2:45). Early church government consisted in the honoring of each believer and in the selection of leaders from among those with special gifts (Acts 6:1–7). In seeking to restore the spirit of the earliest church, which received the Holy Spirit at Pentecost, Presbyterians and all Reformed Christians did not consider that subsequent Christianity got in the way. Reformed Christians admitted that just as all human beings make mistakes, so councils of the church might also err. Nevertheless they affirmed the history of the church and its councils, at least those which formed basic doctrine about the triune nature of God. John Calvin and the rest were quick to affirm the Trinity as an important truth about God.

Already in the sixteenth century, however, some other Protestants who read their Bibles considered the language of the councils at Nicaea and Chalcedon foreign to the words of Scripture. Later, in the early nineteenth century, Thomas Campbell, his son Alexander Campbell, together with followers of another ex-Presbyterian named Barton Stone and some Methodist and Baptist groups, said there was no need for the language of Greek philosophy to confuse the simple words of the Bible. The followers of Barton Stone and the rest began a movement which they called "Christian." Since that time a number of denominations have grown around the world which call themselves "Christian" and "Church of Christ." The best known of these resulted directly from the merger of the Campbellites and the Stoneites—the Christian (Disciples of Christ) Church. To confuse matters further, when the Congregationalist Church in America merged with the Evangelical and Reformed Church in 1957, they called their new, Reformed denomination "The United Church of Christ." Today, when we Presbyterians identify ourselves as "Christians," many mistake us for members of the Disciples, United Church of Christ, or another of the denominations that uses the word in its name. The same holds true for Catholics, Methodists, and Baptists. Just because the word can be misunderstood is no reason to forsake it. In fact, we are all Christians first and foremost; we take our particular denominational names as secondary identities.

Evangelicals All

We Presbyterians, who belong to the Western, Protestant branch of the Christian church, are also almost all evangelicals. We believe that the essence of the faith is the good news that Jesus Christ lived, died, and rose for us. "God so loved the world that he gave his only Son, that whoever believes in him should not perish but have eternal life" (John 3:16). This gospel is the message we seek to live and to proclaim, as Jesus directed disciples to "Go therefore and make disciples of all nations" (Matt. 28:19). This task we enjoy, as do many other kinds of Christians.

In our formal *Book of Order*, we say, "The Church is called to tell the good news of salvation by the grace of God through faith in Jesus Christ as the only Savior and Lord . . . [that] the Church is called to be Christ's faithful evangelist . . . [and that] the Church is called to undertake this mission even at the risk of losing its life" (*Book of Order*, G–3.03–3.04). The *Book of Order* is published as Part II of *The Constitution of the Presbyterian Church (U.S.A.) 1983–85* by the Offices of the General Assembly. Subsequent references to the *Book of Order* refer to the edition cited.) This evangelical center of faith is common among all the Protestant communions historically, and it characterizes Catholic and Eastern branches increasingly.

In America, Presbyterians have almost always considered Reformed churches evangelical in nature. During the nineteenth century, as the voluntary societies such as the American Bible Society, the American Society for Foreign Missions, and the American Tract Society formed, Presbyterians joined with Congregationalists, Methodists, and Baptists to form what they called the "Evangelical United Front." More recently, as we shall see, Presbyterians have led revival movements time and again. In short, Presbyterians have been evangelicals and remain evangelicals.

This point needs to be made in no uncertain terms because some people in the United States today do not consider Presbyterians evangelicals. Just as in the early nineteenth century, some Christians claimed that they alone deserved the term, so in the twentieth others have said that they alone are "evangelicals." By the same token, many Presbyterians have been critical of the hard-sell tactics and vapid teachings of some so-called "evangelicals." But historically and confessionally, Presbyterians have remained evangelicals as surely as we have remained Christians, Protestants, and members of the Reformed family. We have relied on the gospel of Jesus Christ to tell us about the nature of the God we praise.

2

To
Trust
God

. . . He's got the whole world, in his hands.
He's got the whole wide world in his hands.

The congregation had gathered for a family night supper one chilly Spring evening. This one followed the pattern of a Jewish seder meal. Young people had led us in Bible readings and the eating of different symbolic foods. Now as we sat at various tables around the basement, they led us in singing hymns and Christian songs. With the rousing spiritual, we began to clap our hands and raise our voices, "He's got the whole world in his hands." Elsie Robinson, a stalwart, older member of the church whose husband had died just a few months before, bent over toward me and smiled. "Right now," she said, "I know it's true. The world is in God's hands."

To be a Christian, and Elsie Robinson is a good one, means to trust God. Presbyterians emphasize the fact that God gives even the faith to believe in God. In special moments we know, like Elsie Robinson knew, God has the whole world in his hands. "I sought the Lord, and afterward I knew, He moved my soul to seek him seeking me," is the poem of a Christian. It describes the process of faith in profound truth. To believe in Jesus Christ is to trust God, but we know that Christ is not all there is to God.

Historically, Christians have spoken of God as Father, Son and Holy Spirit—one God. Almost every expression of what the Trinity means has at some point in the history of the church been considered heretical. But all agree that God is Creator and provider for all people. Brief words about Trinity, creation, and providence are very important, then, in considering basic Presbyterian beliefs.

God-Triune

Christians from the very beginning recognized that the relation of Jesus Christ to God was a mystery. Jesus spoke of God sometimes as a Being different from himself. When the rich young man called Jesus "Good Teacher," Jesus replied, "Why do you call me good? No one is good but God alone" (Luke 18:18–19). On other occasions, Jesus said that he and God were almost the same (John 12:44–50). When Jesus appeared to his disciples as the resurrected one, he said that he would go to be with God and also that he would be with the believers on earth. In the Acts of the Apostles, the writer says that Jesus told his disciples "not to depart from Jerusalem, but to wait for the promise of the Father . . . before many days you shall be baptized with the Holy Spirit" (Acts 1:4–5). The *Gospel According to Matthew* ends with the command of Jesus to his disciples: "Go therefore, and make disciples of all nations, baptizing them in the name of the Father and of the Son and of the Holy Spirit" (Matt. 28:19).

Very quickly the church developed a doctrine that God was "three in one." This belief that God was triune became, as we have already seen, the major point of contention during most of Christian history. The more leaders tried to spell out the meaning of this mystery, especially as it related to the nature of Christ, the more different traditions emerged. Much of the problem stemmed from the fact that words had different meanings in various parts of the Mediterranean world. Differences among political loyalties and social classes also entered the picture. While almost everyone's Bible possessed the passage from Matthew, the word "Trinity" itself did not occur. More important, many of the philosophical words used to explain the doctrine were foreign to most Christians.

At any rate, when Reformed leaders sought to recapture the spirit and the forms of the early church, they did not quarrel with the creeds which interpreted the meaning of Trinity. John Calvin, who helped articulate much of the Reformed faith, warned Christians not to dismiss the terms about Trinity too quickly. We should recognize that the doctrines were not "rashly invented." By the same token, Calvin declared, we should see how very modestly the great theologians have been regarding it. The "modesty of saintly men ought to warn us against forthwith so severely taking to task, like censors, those who do not wish to swear to the words conceived by us, provided they are not doing it out of either arrogance or forwardness or malicious craft" (*Institutes* I:13, 5).

Subsequently, all of the major Reformed creeds have included the "Trinity," but most have been very modest about spelling out the meaning of the mystery. A classic statement of Trinity can be found in the *Westminster Shorter Catechism*:

> How many Persons are there in the Godhead? There are three Persons in the Godhead: the Father, the Son, and the Holy Ghost; and these three are one God, the same in substance, equal in power and glory.
>
> (*Westminster Shorter Catechism*, Q.A. 6)

The most recently adopted creed, the *Confession of 1967*, says merely that the Trinity is "recognized and reaffirmed as forming the basis and determining the structure of the Christian faith." It speaks of the work of "God, the Father, Son, and Holy Spirit" (*Confession of 1967*, 9.07).

Ninety-nine of a hundred Presbyterians have no difficulty affirming the ancient creeds of the church on Trinity. The creeds represent the wisdom of early Christians, led by the Spirit as the church has been through the ages. Indeed many Presbyterians can even find in the doctrine of Trinity a way of meditating on the mystery of God, as St. Augustine advised many centuries ago. I personally consider the historic creeds beautiful, embodying the faith of other generations and reminding us of our duty to share the faith with people throughout the world who use different tongues and face challenges beyond our own.

What of the Presbyterian who comes from a Baptist or Disciples background where creeds and the doctrine of Trinity have been called hindrances to Christian faith? After all, the word "Trinity" itself is not in the Bible. Such traditions, as well as the Unitarian Church, teach that there is a difference between proclaiming God

Father, Son, and Spirit on one hand, and following the extra-scriptural doctrines of Trinity on the other. Can such people be good Presbyterians? The answer seems to be "Yes."

The new *Book of Order* for the Presbyterian Church (U.S.A.) says, "The congregation shall welcome all persons who respond in trust and obedience to God's grace in Jesus Christ and desire to become part of the membership and ministry of his Church" (*Book of Order*, G–5.0103). Again, active members of the church are those who make a profession of faith in Christ, who are baptized, who have submitted to the government of the church, and who participate in the church's life. Baptism, of course, uses the words from Matthew: "in the name of the Father, and of the Son, and of the Holy Spirit." Elders and deacons in the Presbyterian Church do affirm that we will "receive and adopt the essential tenets of the Reformed faith as expressed in the Confessions of our Church." But the regular member has great latitude in belief on this and other matters. After all, if we truly seek to learn about God, Jesus Christ, and about our own responsibilities in the world, we have already moved a great distance along the path of faith. We trinitarians take such interests as a willingness to learn to be the work of the Spirit, and the work of God the Father we see in creation and providence.

Creator of All

At the bedrock of Reformed faith is the trust in God that God created the universe. God made it all. Presbyterians, who for generations sang only metrical versions of the Psalms, have found great joy in such hymns as these:

> O come, let us sing to the LORD;
>   let us make a joyful noise to the rock of our salvation!
> Let us come into his presence with thanksgiving;
>   let us make a joyful noise to him with songs of praise!
> For the LORD is a great God,
>   and a great King above all gods.
> In his hand are the depths of the earth;
>   the heights of the mountains are his also.
> The sea is his, for he made it;
>   for his hands formed the dry land.
>
> (Psalm 95:1–5)

From Genesis, from the prophets, from the Wisdom writings as well as from the Psalms, we see the power and love of God expressed in creation. Not only did God make the world, the lands, the seas, the stars, the animals, and human beings, God called them all "very good" according to Genesis 1:31. It is increasingly appropriate to affirm God's creation of the universe as our knowledge expands concerning its vast stretches and its minute workings. The faith that God made the world and all the rest enables us to praise God, as did the ancient psalmist.

Some Presbyterians believe honestly that God created the whole universe in just six, twenty-four hour days. Some Presbyterians, myself included, believe that the process of God's creation of the universe began long before the making of life on earth and the fashioning of human beings. I personally see no contradiction between my belief in creation and the theories of evolution which are taught in contemporary scientific disciplines. I am certain, however, that Presbyterians do not have to agree with me on such matters. Nor do I have to agree with the six, twenty-four hour day creationists who say dinosaur bones have been placed on earth to test our faith. In point of fact, we all can see how magnificent the creation is and we can all together praise God for making it (and all of us).

The six day creationists have words from the confessions to back up that point of view. They can also quote the *Westminster Shorter Catechism*, for example: "The work of creation is God's making all things of nothing, by the word of his power, in the space of six days, and all very good" (*Westminster Shorter Catechism*, A.9). Some years ago Presbyterians such as I argued that the word "day" signified a long period of time. Today it seems to me better to say that the essential message of that confession—and all the rest—is not the six days. Rather, it is that God is Creator, and that creation was very good.

In other generations, in both the Presbyterian Church in the U.S.A. and in the Presbyterian Church, U.S., some who believed as I were tried for heresy. Now, however, it seems that Presbyterians are wanting to heal those divisions and allow differences in belief about creation in light of varying backgrounds and interests. The *Book of Order*, for example, says simply that "God created the heavens and the earth and made human beings in God's image, charging them to care for all that lives" (*Book of Order*, G–3.101).

Most important, God the Creator did not "wind up the world" at the beginning of its existence, then just let it go. Presbyterians have consistently linked the creation of the universe with words about God's provident care for it. Again, from the *Book of Order*, comes the statement about the "providence of God who creates, sustains, rules and redeems the world." Every time Presbyterians speak of creation, we naturally follow with a word about providence.

God Cares for All

Jesus, to show the care of God, pointed to some common things: "Look at the birds of the air; they neither sow nor reap nor gather into barns, and yet your heavenly Father feeds them. . . . Consider the lilies of the field. . . . But if God so clothes the grass of the field . . . will he not much more clothe you?" (Matt. 6:26–30). Frequently Jesus talked of God's care for people and for all creation. Jesus and his disciples depended on God's loving care. The general affirmation of God's loving care is called "providence."

Providence speaks of God's care for creation. Therefore, said Calvin, Christian faith has no room for "fortune" or "fate." Fortune, the belief that chance rules sometimes in the world, we express with such notions as "That's the way the cookie crumbles." Fate, a more cruel belief, considers that everyone loses in the end. If fortune is the rolling of some cosmic dice, fate is the rolling of dice always loaded against us. Both fate and fortune indicate a realm of life independent of the rule of God. Reformed faith, at its core, says there is no realm of life outside God's protection and love. So-called "natural occurrences" continue to receive attention from God. Human direction in life comes from God's calling each person into the future.

Reformed faith declares God's providence both from the overwhelming witness of Scripture and from the simplest argument of logic. Both Bible and reason cry "Providence." Abraham, Moses, Deborah, Saul, David, exiled Israelites, Nehemiah, Elizabeth, Mary, Peter, Paul, Cornelius, Lois, Eunice, and Timothy all testify to God's

work in their lives, according to the Bible. These are just a few of
the characters in whom the work of God could be seen.

By the same token, the very definition of God in classical terms
means that God is all-knowing, all-powerful, and everywhere, (om-
niscient, omnipotent, and omnipresent). If God is all-knowing, and
all-powerful, then it follows that God's knowledge of something is
the same as its occurrence. All this is true just from the definitions
of the words, although it can be seen in fact.

Reformed faith, however, has quickly spoken of the mystery in
this process. Human beings do not know, nor can we claim to
manipulate, the secret and majestic providence of God. Why did
God choose the people of Israel as bearers of a special covenant?
Why did God choose to send Jesus Christ as redeemer, the Holy
Spirit as sustainer and comforter? We do not know *how* God's providence works except as God reveals the loving and just outcomes
of it through Scripture and the ongoing creation. We do know *that*
God's providence continues, with a certainty that at times puts in a
shadow knowledge of other matters. That certainty is not perfect
either, as nothing is perfect among human beings. Rather it is the
certainty of faith, especially in times of great need for solace.

Elsie Robinson, who *knew* in that congregational event that
"[God's] got the whole world in his hands," received her faith as a
gift. It is by faith alone, by grace alone, and by Scripture alone that
she can believe in God's creation and God's providence.

3

To Follow Jesus

In the middle of the evening, the phone rang. "Hello, this is Mary Bell," she said. Mary, a longtime member of Anchorage Presbyterian, explained that she wanted help. "They are having a hearing on scattered-site housing next week, and one of the proposed locations is not far from the church. We ought to support this scattered-site if it seems to be good for the poor," she said. "Will you take it to the Care and Outreach Committee. I'll be out of town tomorrow night. Herb and I will be able to go to the hearing next week."

Mary Bell, her husband Herb, and the rest of us at Anchorage Presbyterian Church are trying to follow Jesus in our living. We make commitments with our beliefs; we also make commitments with our actions. Reformed Christians have understood that Christianity is both a belief system and a way of life. To follow Jesus does not mean that we will necessarily favor scattered-site housing in our neighborhood. In fact we had major disagreements on that issue. But Presbyterians since the beginning of our tradition have struggled to make actions and faith consonant with one another.

Personally, I find that sometimes I try harder to follow Jesus than at other times. Mary says she does too. I would suspect that all Presbyterians have more capable and less capable times, that some folks are more disciplined in seeking to follow Jesus than others. Moreover, times change. To follow Jesus has meant different things for Presbyterians in different ages. Today we try also. What guidance do we have as we seek to follow Jesus? We look at the mystery of the nature of Jesus himself, at the work of Jesus for us, and at the process of appropriating trust in God.

The Ministry of Jesus

As Jesus began his ministry, he called to Peter and Andrew, to James and John, and to others: "Come, follow me." Jesus then went about doing good, and he instructed his disciples to "go and do likewise." He also told his followers many things that would help as they attempted to follow him. Following Christ made the Christian as much as did believing certain things about Jesus, God, and the Spirit.

Jesus healed people, for example. He sought their welfare. When friends lowered a paralyzed man through the roof, Jesus healed the man, told him his sins had been forgiven (Luke 5:18–24). Jesus healed a woman with a hemorrhage, the daughter of Jairus, a long time leper, a crazed man, and many others. When a Syrophoenician woman asked Jesus to heal her daughter, he did it and showed that his caring crossed ethnic and racial boundaries (Mark 7:24–30). He cared for everyone, and he sought the welfare of all.

Jesus paid attention to ordinary, human needs—especially the needs of the poor. When crowds came to hear him and to be healed, people became so enthralled with him that they did not leave in order to eat. "Then Jesus called his disciples to him and said, 'I have compassion on the crowd, because they have been with me now three days, and have nothing to eat'" (Matt. 15:32). He produced food for their needs. When a rich young man asked Jesus what he must do to receive eternal life, Jesus told him first to obey the law. Then Jesus, who loved the man, said, "go, sell what you have, and give to the poor, and you will have treasure in heaven; and come, follow me" (Mark 10:17–23).

Jesus also showed his disciples what they should do in order to follow him. They should become trusting, as little children are. They should also heal people where possible. They should give generously to the poor. They should care for the outcasts. At one point, Jesus even said that in caring for the needy, followers would be caring for Jesus himself. "Then the righteous will answer him, 'Lord, when did we see thee hungry and feed thee, or thirsty and give thee drink? And when did we see thee a stranger and welcome thee, or naked and clothe thee? And when did we see thee sick or in prison and visit thee?' And the King will answer them, 'Truly I say to you, as you did it to one of the least of these my brethren, you did it to me'" (Matt. 25:37–40).

In his ministry Jesus fulfilled the law of God. Matthew's Gospel particularly keeps pointing out that Jesus healed and taught "in order to fulfill what was spoken by the prophet" (Matt. 11:14; 13:34). His interpretation of the law differed from that generally understood in his day. He even healed on the sabbath, too, in violation of the rigid laws. In his actions, Jesus showed that God expected obedience in justice and mercy, not in merely doing the prescribed ritual acts of religion. The ministry of Jesus was an all-encompassing life of service and compassion, obedient to God's purpose for people.

Presbyterians, as other Christians, consider that in his death Jesus also ministered. In his death, Jesus also fulfilled the law in accord with God's providence. Jesus prayed, "Father, if thou art willing, remove this cup from me; nevertheless not my will, but thine, be done" (Luke 22:42). When he was crucified, Jesus "became obedient unto death, even death on a cross" (Phil. 2:8). The centurion in charge of the execution and all the rest of the people could see in earthquake and darkness that accompanied the death of Jesus that "Truly, this was a Son of God" (Matt. 27:54).

Jesus, perfectly obedient in life and death, did what no human being had been able to do. Paul and others of the early Christian preachers showed the contrast between the life of Jesus and the lives of others such as Abraham and David (Rom. 4). Most of all, they contrasted the obedience of Adam (and Eve) with the obedience of Jesus Christ. From the very first existence of human beings, sin had been a portion of human experience. Now in Christ Jesus, through faith, people could be freed from the dominion of sin. The ministry of Jesus included dying "for the ungodly." He overcame death's power for believers.

> Therefore as sin came into the world through one man and death through sin, and so death spread to all because all sinned—sin indeed was in the world before the law was given, but sin is not counted where there is no law. Yet death

reigned from Adam to Moses, even over those whose sins
were not like the transgression of Adam, who was a type of
the one who was to come.

(Romans 5:12–14)

Reformed leaders saw Christ's ministry as the beginning of a new
eon in history. They followed a Christian tradition which spoke of
the time before Jesus Christ as under a "covenant of works" and the
time after Christ as a "covenant of grace." Later sections of this
introduction will take up some of the particular parts of this "Covenant theology," as it came to be called. Suffice it to say at this point
simply that it has been important for several strains of Presbyterians.
Many think it still is the most accurate way to speak of the ministry
of Christ. He ushered in the covenant of grace.

Note that in his own ministry, Jesus told followers how to live.
He did not just show them. He said that the traditional law of
religious people did not go far enough in demanding righteousness.
"You have heard it said . . . 'You shall not kill. . . . ' But I say to
you that every one who is angry with his brother shall be liable to
judgment" (Matt. 5:21–22). Jesus reinterpreted others of the Ten
Commandments, and others of the laws, so that people could see
God demanded wholehearted obedience in mind and spirit as well
as in deed.

When that rich young man came to Jesus he was told first to
obey the regular law. Then Jesus called for further obedience. When
Jesus taught about justice, he called for believers to go beyond
merely paying back debts or doing their duty. "You have heard that
it was said, 'An eye for an eye and a tooth for a tooth.' But I say to
you, Do not resist one who is evil. But if anyone strikes you on the
right cheek, turn to him the other also" (Matt. 5:38–39). "Go the
extra mile." "Pray for those who persecute you." On and on the
commands of Christ called for followers to be more like Jesus himself.

The Atonement

Even though Mary Bell and all the rest of us are trying to follow
Jesus, we realize that we cannot obey perfectly the law of God.
Only through the life and death of Jesus Christ have we participated
in full obedience. Though some Christian traditions today empha-

size only the example of Jesus in living, most including the Presbyterian still consider the death of Jesus as a center of that ministry for us.

Just how we are reconciled to God through the work of Jesus Christ has been the subject of great debate. All the various images or theories of the ways Jesus worked to reconcile and of the "atonement" came from the Bible. Was Jesus the moral example, living and dying that others might see how to live and die? Was Jesus the payment by God of a kind of ransom to the powers of sin and death, so that believers could be freed from those powers? Was Jesus the cosmic victor over the evil one, whose armies had controlled the world since the beginning of history, subject only to the overarching powers of God? Was Jesus the substitution of a guiltless victim for the guilty ones (people) to satisfy God's own justice? Again, all of these theories had bases in Scripture. Reformed theologians have not usually denied the truth of any of them.

Reformed Christians, however, have generally depended on the image of Jesus Christ, the substitute for human beings, in considering the nature of the atonement. In Calvin's *Institutes*, the question is asked, "What . . . would Christ have bestowed upon us if the penalty for our sins were still required?" The answer, following 1 Peter 2:24 and other portions of Scripture, is that "Lo, you see plainly that Christ bore the penalty of sins to deliver his own people from them" (*Institutes* III: 4, 30). In the feisty words of the *Scots Confession*, "[We believe] that our Lord Jesus offered himself a voluntary sacrifice unto his Father for us, that he suffered contradiction of sinners, that he was wounded and plagued for our transgressions, that he, the clean innocent Lamb of God, was condemned in the presence of an earthly judge, that we should be absolved before the judgment seat of our God" (*Scots Confession*, 3.09).

Human Sin

The ministry of Christ and his atonement show just how much we need both. Presbyterians historically have paid a great deal of attention to the Bible's teachings that "all have sinned and fallen short of the glory of God" (Rom. 3:23). The doctrine has been called "total depravity." By this Presbyterians and other Calvinists have meant that every part of the human being is affected by sin. Every act continues tinged by sin. No person, no action can be entirely free from sin. Only Jesus Christ lived, died, and rose as an exception to this universal sinfulness.

Presbyterians in former centuries took some pleasure in this doctrine of total depravity, it must be admitted. However, more recently the various Presbyterian churches have modified the most blatant statements of it, along with some of the other "harsh" words of traditional Calvinism. But still nothing done in this world is perfect, according to Presbyterian confessions.

Take the example of scattered-site housing, which has presented itself recently for our community. Every action, including the one "deciding" to do nothing about providing adequate housing for the poor, contains inevitable sin. Even a creative and viable solution to a human situation calls forth self-righteousness, or some other proud feeling. The self-interest of builders, speculators, bureaucrats, church-people, and many others will be involved in the situation. In brief, Mary Bell and I, who will favor the proposal, the people opposing it, and those who want to take no action will all be involved in human sin. So will our communities, our social systems, and our churches that own property. That is the condition of human depravity which confessions say has existed since the very first human beings lived.

As the study moves along, we shall return to the subject of human sin. Right now it is important to see it as a belief which is related to our attempts to follow Jesus. It helps us understand the Reformed teachings about God's work to bring us into the communion of saints. It helps put in perspective what we mean when we promise to follow Jesus and depend on him alone. That process of salvation, in traditional words "the economy of redemption," also pertains to the following of Jesus.

Effectual Calling

Presbyterians spent considerable energy working out a vocabulary to describe the process of appropriation of atonement. "Effectual calling" was just one of their terms. Others have included: "justification," "repentance," "adoption," and "sanctification." It is significant that all these words came originally from the Bible, and they represented a logical progression as well. All the process began and remained God's gift, and human beings could do nothing outside of God's gifts to start it or to speed it along. These are traditional terms used to describe the process in which we have become followers of Jesus, realizing that we cannot do what Jesus did.

Effectual calling means that God does the work in permitting us to believe and to try following Jesus. In the words of the *Westminster Shorter Catechism*, "Effectual calling is the work of God's Spirit, whereby, convincing us of our sin and misery, enlightening our minds in the knowledge of Christ, and renewing our wills, he doth persuade and enable us to embrace Jesus Christ, freely offered to us in the gospel" (*Westminster Shorter Catechism*, A.31). In the words of Paul, it is the "spirit of wisdom and of revelation" which enlightens "the eyes of your hearts" so "that you may know what is the hope to which he has called you" (Eph. 1:18).

In the sequence of trying to follow Jesus we are first enabled to repent, to recognize the sinfulness in which we exist and call upon God for forgiveness. We are then permitted to sense that God does not count our sin against us, because Christ intercedes for us. Then we experience the falling away of sin, the restoring of our relationship as children of God. Finally, we move in the process of following Jesus.

4

To Live
in the Spirit

When Dick Hays approached me at coffee time, I could tell he had a question on his mind. "Before we go upstairs to worship, can you tell me about the charismatics?"

"Well, Dick," I responded, "what do you want to know?"

"We were reading Acts in Sunday school. What happened when the Spirit came? Are we Presbyterians just as able to have gifts of the Spirit as those early church folk? And do the charismatics have them?"

Dick Hays always asks good questions, usually much deeper than a coffee-break response can plumb. Today questions about the nature and teachings of the Holy Spirit come from longtime Presbyterians such as he. They come even more quickly from Christians who have been members of Holiness or Pentecostal churches and now belong to a Presbyterian body.

There are many ways to speak about the work of the Holy Spirit. Reformed leaders have considered the Bible telling about the Spirit as "proceeding from the Father and the Son," as the agent of sanctification, as the giver of authority, and as the power of God for reconciliation. The gifts of the Spirit are important to mention also.

Proceeding from Father and Son

The Gospels are full of references to the Spirit as coming from God. In the accounts of the birth of Jesus Christ, for example, the statements about Mary's conception refer to the Holy Spirit (Matt. 1:18; Luke 1:35). In the accounts of Jesus being baptized by John, the Spirit of God descended "like a dove." The voice from heaven said, "This is my beloved Son, with whom I am well pleased" (Matt. 3:16). When Jesus sent out disciples for the first time, he told them not to worry. "The Spirit of your Father" would speak through them (Matt. 10:20). Words from the prophets fulfilled by actions of Jesus included those from Isaiah about the servant with God's Spirit "upon him" (Matt. 12:18).

Again, almost as many passages spoke of the Spirit coming from Jesus Christ himself. Jesus was perceived as "full of the Holy Spirit" (Luke 4:1). After his resurrection, Jesus appeared to his disciples and said "Peace be with you." Then he breathed on them and said "Receive the Holy Spirit" (John 20:22). He promised his Spirit, the Comforter, would be with disciples, and early leaders considered the Spirit as being from Jesus Christ as well as from God the Father.

It seems that through much of Christian history, people did not work as hard on developing the doctrines about the Holy Spirit as they did on the doctrines about Christ. For the most part, they simply confirmed the standard creeds. The creed from Constantinople (A.D. 381) had said that the church believed in the "Holy Spirit, the Lord and Giver of life . . . who proceeds from the Father and the Son . . . Who is worshipped and glorified together with the Father and the Son, who spoke through the prophets."

Even this much doctrine has caused splits among Christians. Some said the Spirit could not proceed from the Son as from the Father. For most Christians it has been simple to think of God as Transcendent Creator on the one hand, and as Incarnate Redeemer on the other. This third person of the Trinity could not be put in a logical place, although most Protestants have kept a doctrine of the Spirit somewhere in their minds. Both Disciples of Christ and Presbyterians at certain times tended to downplay the divinity of the Holy Spirit as a distinct entity within the Godhead.

In the twentieth century, both the Presbyterian Church U.S.A. and the Presbyterian Church, U.S., took the trouble to amend the *Westminster Confession of Faith* in order to include chapters on the Holy Spirit.

In revising the creed, Presbyterians emphasized this ancient word that the Spirit *proceeds* from Father and Son. They said also, with the early church leaders, that the Holy Spirit should receive faith, love, obedience, and praise with the other persons of Trinity. However, contemporary Presbyterians also emphasized that the Holy Spirit is active in the work of redemption. They likewise told of the work of the Spirit in uniting believers in the church universal.

Agent of Sanctification

In the work of redemption, the Holy Spirit is the grace of God calling people from sinful, self-centered lives, into worship and praise of God. Paul spoke of the Spirit ushering in God's new relationship with people:

> For the law of the Spirit of life in Christ Jesus has set me free from the law of sin and death. . . . For those who live according to the flesh set their minds upon the things of the flesh, but those who live according to the Spirit set their minds on the things of the Spirit. To set the mind on the flesh is death, but to set the mind on the Spirit is life and peace.
> (Romans 8:2, 5–6)

Through the Spirit come regeneration, repentance, adoption, and freedom in Christ. Through the Spirit comes the will to "be perfect, as your heavenly Father is perfect" (Matt. 5:48). Through the Spirit comes even prayer itself, intercession with God in behalf of ourselves and others.

If sin persists in the lives of believers, how does the Spirit yield freedom, holiness, and prayer? Presbyterians have affirmed that God makes believers better than they had been. Just because we cannot in this life be perfect does not excuse us from doing our best to follow Jesus, to live in the Spirit. What is begun in this life God completes for the faithful. We pay close attention to the examples of Simon Peter, the Apostle Paul, and others in that early church. None of them became perfect, we say, although a number were heroic Christians.

Paul wrote almost constantly of the work of the Spirit in his own process of "putting on Christ," his process of sanctification. Yet Paul realized that he continued to sin. It was in that context that Paul told early Christians that he was being "sanctified by the Holy Spirit" (Rom. 15:16).

Both Catholics and members of the Holiness wing of the Methodist movement have different views about the sanctifying work of the Holy Spirit. The Catholic Church has traditionally taught that God gives special gifts to some Christians through the Spirit. When believers cooperate with those gifts more merit is created than necessary for the salvation of that particular believer. The extra merit becomes available for other Christians who need it. All the good comes from God; but with the special saints sharing, they intercede for us. This very complex doctrine, developed over centuries of theology, contrasts somewhat with Presbyterian reliance on God's Spirit (grace) alone. Both points of view have basis in Scripture, and today we see more in common than different about the Spirit's agency in behalf of sanctification.

The Holiness wing in Methodism, developing through the nineteenth century among different Protestant denominations, teaches that any believer can be perfect in this life. While the United Methodist Church and other mainstream denominations would not make such bold statements, the founder of Methodism, John Wesley, did say Christians needed to hear Christ's command: "Be perfect." Wesley and the Methodist tradition doubtless helped Presbyterians in the eighteenth century and, more recently, opened up discussion of the nature of the Holy Spirit. But Holiness communions accused Catholics, Presbyterians, and regular Methodists of being lazy and only half trusting the power of the Spirit to make people perfect.

Presbyterians, in dialogue with other bodies in reforming our own thought, have grown to say more about the Spirit in recent decades. Some Presbyterians might even believe people can be perfect in this life, but a vast majority of us believe that life in the Spirit does not rule out the fact that we continue to sin within this life. We see God empowering us to grow in faith, to make more mature decisions, and to live more faithfully. We see the Holy Spirit providing Christian freedom in which we can live, but we do not view ourselves as perfect. Personally, I take solace and energy from this belief. I fully expect other Presbyterians, including Dick Hays, do too.

Giver of Authority

Presbyterians also believe that the Holy Spirit provides authority for the believer. The Spirit, for example, enabled the writers of

Scripture to tell truthfully about God, Jesus Christ, and all the rest of
the things necessary for us to know. We say the Bible writers were
"in-*spired*" by the *Spirit*. We believe that the same Spirit enables us
to read and interpret the Bible for ourselves in community. In the
famous words of John Calvin, it is the "inward witness of the Holy
Spirit" that seals biblical authority for us.

Though a few may have sounded like they believed it, no Presbyterians I know have ever argued that the Bible by magic could
answer all things with full certainty for the believer. On the other
hand, no Presbyterian I know has said the Bible is "just another
book." Presbyterians want to stress that God's Spirit gives the Bible
its power to help and to teach us. The church does not give the
Bible power, rather the Bible, as interpreted through the Spirit, gives
the church power.

As the Spirit gives authority in the writing and reading of Scripture, so it also gives authority to the church. Presbyterians believe
that church councils, confessions, and assemblies can err. But they
still have more authority than does the isolated Christian. Though
God alone is Lord of the conscience, Christians are to realize the
power of the Spirit working within the life of the church. Such a
realization brings modesty. The Christian can be made "teachable,"
ready to grow in grace, with humility and a willingness to listen to
the true church.

In fact, the Holy Spirit gives authority to all powers recognized
on earth for good. In the words of the *Westminster Confession of
Faith* as amended earlier in this century:

> By the indwelling of the Holy Spirit all believers being
> vitally united to Christ, who is the head, are thus united one
> to another in the Church, which is his body. He calls and
> anoints ministers for their holy office, qualifies all other of-
> ficers in the Church for their special work, and imparts var-
> ious gifts and graces to its members. He gives efficacy to the
> Word and to the ordinances of the gospel. By him the Church
> will be preserved, increased, purified, and at last made per-
> fectly holy in the presence of God.
>
> (*Westminster Confession of Faith*, 6.171)

This statement ties together nicely the Reformed understanding
of the Holy Spirit providing authority with the corporate nature of

the church. It also affirms that the Holy Spirit gives various gifts, a response to the question from Dick Hays.

Giver of Gifts

The Apostle Paul spoke eloquently about the gifts of the Spirit. "To one is given through the Spirit the utterance of wisdom, to another the utterance of knowledge according to the same Spirit, to another faith by the same Spirit, to another gifts of healing by the one Spirit, to another the working of miracles, to another prophecy, to another the ability to distinguish between spirits, to another various kinds of tongues, to another the interpretation of tongues" (1 Cor. 12:8–10). Each of the gifts has been given for the common good, as each part of the body helps the whole.

At several points Paul made lists of what he called "the fruits of the Spirit." In one place he said, "the fruit of the Spirit is love, joy, peace, patience, kindness, goodness, faithfulness, gentleness, self-control" (Gal. 5:22). Presbyterians have seen all these as gifts of the Holy Spirit. The Holy Spirit also gives each person a sense of "calling" to a special function in the world, in keeping with God's providence and Christ's summons to "follow him." In these ways, Presbyterians have consistently been "charismatics." We have been consciously dependent on the *charisma*, the *charismata*, from God—God's Spirit's gifts.

In recent years, as at several previous times in Christian history, speaking in tongues has become important for many Christians. This phenomenon occurred during the great revivals of the early nineteenth century, for example, along with other physical symptoms of religious experience. Presbyterians in those days generally discouraged believers from speaking in tongues and from other "spiritual exercises," as they called them. In this twentieth-century movement, Presbyterians have reacted in a more positive manner. Now several thousands of Presbyterians who speak in tongues feel that they have an important place in the church. Presbyterians who speak in tongues consider that the Holy Spirit gives the gift, as other gifts. In some congregations factions have arisen between those speaking in tongues and those with other commitments. In other congregations, however, differing persuasions have found mutual goals and worship together.

A Presbyterian may speak in tongues, but certainly none has to. By the same token, a Presbyterian may feel uncomfortable with fellow worshipers speaking in tongues. Indeed, the same thing may be true for many other aspects of congregational worship and life. As long as the other gifts of the Spirit are present—utterance of wisdom, utterance of knowledge, faith, and the like—Presbyterians can make good accounting of the gifts of tongues and interpretations of tongues. And the important thing is the fruit of the Spirit—love, joy, peace, patience, and all the rest.

5

To
Walk
in the Way

Sunday morning. End of the summer. Our minister, John Ames, rose to stand in the pulpit as he led worship. Already that morning we had participated in the baptism of Priya Anne Alexander, infant daughter of Suraj and Rachel who belong to Anchorage Presbyterian Church. The Alexanders are now Presbyterian, but they grew up in the Mar Thoma Church and the Syrian Orthodox Church in India. John drew our attention to their history as he read the Scripture and preached: "He Knows Our Name, Too."

One Scripture lesson came from Exodus 3, the passage in which Moses receives the call from God to rescue the people of Israel from oppression.

> Then Moses said to God, "If I come to the people of Israel and say to them, 'The God of your fathers has sent me to you,' and they ask me 'What is his name?' what shall I say to them?" God said to Moses, "I AM WHO I AM." And he said, "Say this to the people of Israel, 'I AM has sent me to you.'"
> (Exodus 3:13–14)

The other lesson came from the Gospel of John, chapter 17, in which Jesus prayed for his disciples and for the church: "Holy Father, keep them in thy name, which thou hast given me, that they may be one even as we are one. While I was with them, I kept them in thy name, which thou hast given me" (John 17:11, 12). Then, John Ames began to preach.

His sermon, as usual, dealt with the passages of Scripture. He explained how the people of Israel used the sacred letters signifying

God, how God remained faithful to them, and how Jesus called God "Daddy" in intimate terms. He related it to the baptism of Priya Anne and to the education of children for growth in faith. He also told us about our belonging to the family of God—how we are entrusted with the raising of children so they know God, too.

The sermon, the Scripture lessons, the baptism, and the whole worship service were together a part of our "walking in the way" of the Christian faith as Presbyterians. We consider that the worship, the sacraments, the proclamation of the Word of God, and the gathering of the congregation are all important for us. Distinctive for Presbyterians is the preaching and hearing of the Word, a necessary part of our being disciples. But the whole experience fits in one piece with the life we lead as a portion of our obedience.

The early church at times called their new life "The Way." Early Christians followed the Bible, by which they meant the books of the Old Testament. These, together with the changes and the new instruction of "The Way," (writings that have become for us the New Testament) led the Christians in discipleship. We have already looked briefly at the authority of Scripture, but let us note now the authority of the Reformed tradition and the leadership of the church for teaching us "The Way" of discipleship. What is the meaning of discipleship in the church?

The Presbyterian Way

Gradually, one wing of Protestants in the sixteenth century came to practice representative government. Members of this Reformed wing, with special emphases in theology already mentioned and special beliefs about sacraments and the nature of law yet to be discussed, also agreed that certain forms of church government followed Scripture. They saw themselves as heirs to the biblical patterns of government, and they saw these patterns as helpful for those seeking to be disciples in their own day.

Presbyterians have considered representative government, the selection of elders especially, as a process faithful to the organization of ancient Israel as well as that of the early church. The Old Testament spoke often of elders, and the Jewish communities had elders in the time of Jesus Christ. Presbyterians note the appointment of elders in local congregations (Acts 14:23), their selection of Paul and Barnabas, and the role of elders in the council at Jerusalem. Why, the Pastoral epistles even told what kind of person should be an elder! A leader should "not be arrogant or quick-tempered or a drunkard or violent or greedy for gain, but hospitable, a lover of goodness, master of himself, upright, holy, and self-controlled" (Titus 1:7–9). From the Greek word for "elder," *presbuteros*, came the name for Presbyterians, "those ruled by elders." Presbyterian pioneers considered the word "elder" a synonym in the New Testament for the word "Bishop," a word of importance for Catholic, Anglican, and Methodist Christians among others. Presbyterians since the time of John Calvin have considered that some elders need to be trained for proclamation of the Word especially, while others need to be in all kinds of Christian vocations as lay leaders. The teaching elders, or ministers, and the ruling elders, or lay leaders, should share power in the church. Though Presbyterian denominations have developed differently in various countries, this accent on shared leadership has remained remarkably consistent.

Leaders chosen from the local congregation as ruling elders, together with a teaching elder, or minister, govern the local, or "particular" church. Elders of both kinds form a presbytery, a court governing the life of congregations in a local area. Representatives from various presbyteries comprise a synod, a regional court. And representatives from all the presbyteries in a denomination gather for a General Assembly.

As congregations and church courts have become more complex in our own country, other people have been selected by various courts to be responsible for particular programs or meeting certain needs—in missions, for example, or in evangelism. In addition, as local churches have grown, many have called more than one minister to serve them. The size and complexity of Presbyterianism has demanded the adoption of many rules for congregations, church courts, ministers, and leaders. The *Book of Order* in large measure spells out the "Presbyterian Way" of representative government in our denomination.

We Presbyterians do not have to believe in this "Presbyterian Way" in the same way we believe in God. In fact, wise Presbyterians through the centuries have recognized that other Christians can be just as faithful following different forms of government, whether congregational or episcopal. No, we just have to practice this "Presbyterian Way" of living in community. Personally, I have found representative church government frustrating at times, but I have grown to love the way in which God's Spirit seems to permit courts to rise above differences in beliefs and opinions to unite in integrated work and worship.

We Presbyterians believe church courts are not perfect, just as we believe Christians are not perfect in this life. But we understand that representative courts can sometimes check the errors of individuals. As the whole church of God is a community—one body of Christ—so the representatives of the larger church usually embody the wisdom of Christ better than do solitary believers. When selected as representatives to church courts, we should serve with care and diligence. When our presbytery speaks, or our General Assembly, we should listen. And we realize that the *Book of Order* can be changed in accord with the wills of Assemblies and presbyteries.

Some years ago, for example, Presbyterian leaders in all major denominations in the United States came to see that women should share in the formal government of the church and in the proclamation of the word. Gradually editions of the *Book of Order* were changed first to permit women to organize their own areas of leadership and work in local churches, then to permit women to address church bodies, then to permit the ordination of women as teaching and ruling elders, and now to urge church courts fairly to select women in accord with female membership in the church. Personally, it seemed the various changes took place far too slowly. But I know others in the church who think the changes occurred much too rapidly. Yet we all remain committed to the representative form of government, which moves in organic fashion to respond to God's will in changing situations.

We Presbyterians follow the "Presbyterian Way" in our attempts to be faithful disciples of Jesus Christ. In following Jesus, we really become disciples to the Master.

Discipleship

Life in the early church was filled with worship, service, and education. Notice how much the early church remembered worship, and the power of the sermons in worship. Peter preached at Pentecost, when the Holy Spirit gave power to the disciples. In the course of worship and fasting, the Christian elders in Antioch made their decision to send Paul and Barnabas as missionaries (Acts 13:2). Eutychus even fell from the upper window when he slept during worship and he received healing from the Apostles (Acts 20:9).

Naturally one of the elements in discipleship involves a commitment to attend worship. Presbyterians do not have rules about attending worship. If people fail to show any commitment, then the leaders of a Presbyterian congregation have a responsibility to put their names on an inactive role. But no one has to go to worship. On the other hand, the center of worship is praise of God and instruction in "The Way." What better way is a Presbyterian led in learning about God and about the faith than in worship?

Perhaps more significant than merely being there in worship is the active listening and participation expected of members in Presbyterian churches. Discipleship involves keeping one's ears open especially to the reading of Scripture, to the proclamation of the Word, and to the celebration of the sacraments. I guess it is more properly put to "keep one's heart and mind open." In the sermon John Ames preached, we could learn a great deal about the nature of God, about the transmission of the faith, and about our own responsibilities. Those teachings seem to me implicit in the Scripture itself, but John brought them out for us to hear and understand.

There is a pattern of Presbyterian worship, based in part on the Western liturgy of the Roman Catholic Church from which we have come. Also a part of our tradition is the reading of Scripture in the language of the people, the preaching of a sermon that explains the Scripture and applies it for our lives, and the singing of hymns of praise. We also engage in public prayer, with words formed for us by the minister and other worship leaders. Patterns of worship change, but they remain rather consistent at the same time. These patterns are described in the *Directory for the Service of God* that like the

Book of Order possesses authority for us. It describes the ways in which Anchorage Presbyterian Church and all the other congregations should render worship. John Ames, our minister, Mary Morgan, our associate minister, the session, and all the rest of us use the *Directory for the Service of God* as a guide for our corporate worship.

Obviously, discipleship involves worship and a great deal more. For Reformed Christians service in worship is preparation for service in the world. Our discipleship involves proclaiming the gospel as well as we can in whatever we do. Now that is a full time job! Being a member of "The Way" means that we listen to Jesus' words:

> "You are the light of the world. A city set on a hill cannot be hid. Nor do people light a lamp and put it under a bushel, but on a stand, and it gives light to all in the house. Let your light so shine before [people], that they may see your good works and give glory to your Father who is in heaven."
> (Matthew 5:14–16)

Discipleship, then, means that we Presbyterians are to "let our light shine." Sometimes this means we invite others to join us in worship. Sometimes it means that we actually go to other communities and other lands to serve Jesus Christ by helping people there learn about God. Sometimes it means we have to take an unpopular stand in work, school, or social groups. Sometimes it means we help people simply because they need help—they are hungry, thirsty, in prison, or strangers.

Discipleship has all kinds of meaning for us. How can we know what should be done or said? In many cases we look to the Bible for instruction. We also look to the tradition of the church, not just to follow what has been done before but to learn in our own day what it means to be obedient. We follow the leading of those who have preceded us. We look to the leaders of the Presbyterian Church, speaking through General Assemblies and other courts. All the while we realize our discipleship will not be perfect. God saves us by grace, through faith—not by judging the life we lead. Still we try to "let our light shine" so people seeing us will "give God the glory."

Discipline

Presbyterians have a special tradition of exercising church discipline. In earlier times, on the American frontier, for example, church courts dealt with matters of social concern and commerce. I enjoy telling about the minutes of one presbytery in which a minister was brought to trial for selling a horse to an elder. The minister alleged the horse was healthy, but the animal died a few days later. More serious were church court cases dealing with abuse of slaves, with immorality among elders, and with people engaging in "unhealthy work." Sometimes the cases seemed unfair, such as the one in South Carolina where a telephone operator was disciplined for having to work on Sunday. Often, though, the cases helped Presbyterians understand in real terms that being a disciple involved discipline. It "is exercised within the context of pastoral care and oversight," by its very nature (*Rules of Discipline*, D-1.01. The *Rules of Discipline* are published as part of the *Book of Order*, prepared by the Joint Committee on Presbyterian Union. Subsequent references to the *Rules of Discipline* refer to the edition cited.)

Church discipline among Presbyterians follows the *Rules of Discipline*, another adopted statement with authority for those of us in the denomination. The *Rules of Discipline* look like those of any formal body. They exist to permit structures for dissent, to specify jurisdiction, and to regulate discipline of members and courts of the church. In extreme cases, members can even be expelled from the church. Almost all the time, however, church discipline merely stands as a possibility for redress as the church goes about its business. After all, the business of the church (as the business of believers) is love of God and neighbors. In the Presbyterian Church, love of neighbor remains exceedingly important.

6

To
Love
Your Neighbor

"Room for me, too?" Jean Elliot hopped on the bus. Louis Coleman, Director of the Presbyterian Community Center, began explaining to us about its functions as we rode together to see it. Our Sunday school class, with Mrs. Elliot and several other interested members of the wider congregation, took a Sunday afternoon to learn about needs at the center, things we could do to help. The Rademaker family, the Gillises, the Milwoods, the Cunninghams, the Perkeys, the Troys, Bob Hawkes, and several more of us ate lunch together, boarded the school bus, and toured the center.

"This child care center is the jewel of our program, now." Louis showed us around; and then introduced us to Mrs. Davis, who directs that program. "With the drying up of government money, the church's contribution will be more crucial," Mrs. Davis told us. She said many families simply leave their young children with unskilled and uninterested residents in the nearby public housing project. "We really need support to enable families to bring their young children here," Louis Coleman explained.

As we met afterwards, our class decided to help support children at the Presbyterian Community Center as a special project in addition to the gifts we give through presbytery for the center.

"We ought to be able to give at least thirty-five dollars a week for this," Bruce Rademaker declared. We nodded. We reached in our pockets. We told other class members, and they contributed too.

Anchorage Presbyterian Church is not too big, but we manage to support lots of causes with our time, skills, and money. Members lead a "Studio for the Handicapped" program that provides well-constructed materials for public school children who cannot read regular texts, cassettes of articles and books not available elsewhere for the visually handicapped, and an FM station with special programming. Some members are especially interested in an interdenominational mission that houses street people, others in a Salvation Army project, and still others in a college in eastern Kentucky for young people from the mountain area. Some members drive vans to deliver meals to shut-ins. A number of women help female inmates in a prison ministry. At least two of the members of Anchorage serve in a Youth Advocates program, which seeks to meet special needs of young offenders. One elder last summer spent her vacation working as a nurse in rural Haiti. On and on the list goes of members in our local church caring and helping, in personal ways and in support of worthwhile institutions.

Right next door to the church building is Bellewood Presbyterian Home for Children, a co-op-presbytery-sponsored place for families to receive help and for children to reside when necessary. Many other churches in our area help in other ways. And through our presbytery, synod, and General Assembly we are connected in a network of caring that touches almost every portion of the earth. That is nothing peculiar to Presbyterians, but it is an essential part of being a Presbyterian. Individually, and together, we Presbyterians try to love our neighbors as Jesus told us to.

Christian Care

When a lawyer asked Jesus, "Teacher, what must I do to inherit eternal life?" Jesus replied that a person should love God with everything, "and your neighbor as yourself." The inquirer responded with another, serious question: "Who is my neighbor?"

Jesus responded with a story of compassion and care. He told the lawyer of a traveler, mugged and left half-dead on the road. A priest passed him by, as did a member of the elite class in society, but a Samaritan, member of a despised class in Palestine at the time, stopped and gave personal care. He carried the victim to an inn and paid for his lodging. Jesus asked, "Which of these three, do you think, proved neighbor?" (Luke 10:29–37).

Elsewhere in the Gospels Jesus had many things to say about the responsibility of believers to care for the needy. He said the blessed would be separated from the cursed on the basis of their care for the little people in the world. He said he would not forget even the person who gave a cup of cold water. He himself helped people right and left.

Obviously, the believer should "go and do likewise," as Jesus said on several occasions. Christians immediately began to care for one another and for others in need. The record of the church may contain many inglorious moments, but it uniformly shows Christians care for the needy. In the forming of the Presbyterian wing of the church, pioneers took pains to provide care for the poor. Every strain of the Reformed tradition has maintained care for the needy among its priorities.

Presbyterian care is both individual and structural. Do hungry people need food? Presbyterians in many communities including our own participate in local grocery closets, metropolitan-wide efforts to meet emergencies, and legislative attempts to improve the system for people to find jobs and food. At the same time, we Presbyterians through our denominational and ecumenical channels supply vital food for hungry people in Africa, Asia, and Latin America. And we assist in the establishment of demonstration farms in poverty areas which show farmers how to improve production for themselves. This emphasis on both the simple and the complex typifies Presbyterian caring.

Nevertheless, many Presbyterians differ in the ways they choose to help. Some even contend against legislative support for the poor, for example. A few consider meeting individual needs in some countries as a contribution to the problem rather than a solution. All Presbyterians do not agree on the proper methods of helping the poor. Yet one cannot be a practicing Presbyterian type of Christian without caring and trying in some way to "love neighbor as self." That command of Jesus profoundly affects our response to human need.

What is true in the matters of hunger and food also is true in other matters. What about Presbyterian positions on touchy ethical concerns such as environmental protection, abortion, and peace-making? Do Presbyterians have to believe certain ways about these matters, as some other communions demand?

Christian care, Presbyterian style does not demand certain points of view on some ethical issues. Some Presbyterians support "Right to Life" organizations while others support "Freedom-of-Choice" alternatives. Some Presbyterians serve in the armed forces, while others take a thorough, pacifist stance on war and military armies. Some consider the needs of people more important than environmental considerations; others feel protection of the air, water, and resources come first in behalf of future generations.

To move into deep exploration of these issues and Presbyterian styles of ethical action would demand another whole book. We do grapple seriously with the complex nature of such issues, and this prohibits most Presbyterians from taking an absolute position on them. By the same token, all decisions and actions are not equally Christian from our perspectives. Our confessions speak of our being able to do "good works," not entirely pure and unselfish but "acceptable" nonetheless. Certain obvious guidelines help us in some responses to neighbors, and assemblies of the church help in addressing others.

Bible and Caring

In the very first chapter, I promised to deal with the relationship of belief and practice: how do beliefs about God, Jesus Christ, the Spirit, and the church affect values and decision-making? Well, some general principles have become clear. Jesus explained who neighbors are, for example. The Bible clearly indicates, and we Presbyterians believe, that neighbors include all people. Even those who might be considered "enemies" by some group to which we belong are no longer enemies for us as we seek to follow Christ. "Love your enemies," said Jesus Christ. "Pray for those who persecute you" (Matt. 5:44). We may not be able in immature faith to act upon this clear command of Christ. In fact at times whole Presbyterian churches have failed to follow the precept and the universal meaning of "neighbor." These failures in the past do not mean that God intends us to keep on in disobedience. Do we have faith in God, seek to follow Christ, trust life in the Spirit? Then we move to more universal caring about neighbor, more thorough prayer for all people. A friend suggested our program as Presbyterians might be "to enlarge the O.K.O.P." He said that means enlarging our ideas of "Our Kind of People." The Bible says that process goes on until we include all.

Again, the Bible is extremely clear about some values—justice, for example. God had been seen long before the coming of Christ as a "just God," interested in the people of Israel keeping justice before themselves. To exercise justice was to honor God. "The LORD of Hosts is exalted in justice," said Isaiah, "and the Holy God shows himself holy in righteousness" (Isa. 5:17). Isaiah warned against turning the phrases to subvert the value: "Woe to those who call evil good and good evil, who put darkness for light and light for darkness, who put bitter for sweet and sweet for bitter!" (Isa. 5:20). No, the justice in most cases is plain. Jeremiah, Ezekiel, Micah, and all the rest agreed. The problems in perceiving what would be just came mostly from "hard hearts" among the people.

Much of what we would consider mercy the Old Testament takes as a part of justice. According to Isaiah, God told the people of Israel: "cease to do evil, learn to do good; seek justice, correct oppression; defend the fatherless, plead for the widow" (Isa. 1:16–17). People were to harvest fields with justice, that is they were to leave the edges standing so the poor would have something to eat. All this and more was just within the realm of justice. But Micah said God required the faithful to "do justice, love mercy." He spelled it out perhaps just in case there might be a question about the limits of justice.

Jesus, as we all know, extended the limits of justice. Christians were to go the extra mile, give the cloak and coat, too. Christians were to keep on forgiving. Justice was to be extended to all, not to mention the giving of mercy to everyone.

In our own day, in these United States, applications of values of justice and mercy are readily apparent for Presbyterians who take the trouble to notice. Discrimination based on skin color, gender, and age cannot be just. Some ethical issues might be thorny; but one of the thorniest is basic justice for Black people, Hispanics, Asian refugees, women, older folks, children, and other groups.

What Presbyterian can ignore the obvious need to seek justice for all these people? In fact, the great majority of us who are Presbyterians have tasted discrimination as members of one or more of these groups. The honest truth for us, however, is that most Americans who suffer the worst discrimination are not Presbyterians. We can love justice and seek mercy in their behalf.

Again, we Presbyterians affirm our growth in the body of Christ. If the Bible speaks clearly on matters of justice and mercy, and if we seek to do justice and to love mercy, we believe we can be led by God's Spirit from the more clear cut issues into the more complex. This principle John Calvin and other Reformed theologians have repeated again and again, especially in matters of biblical interpretation. Be guided by the simple and the clear. We have plenty of work to do if we begin with what we clearly know is fair, just, and merciful. In addition, we can rely upon our fellow Christians to provide us with guidance in meeting ethical issues.

Caring and the Assembly

Many particular issues, in which we seek to "love our neighbor," do not have specific and obvious answers from the Bible. Our information on them seems mixed, and no clear word about right and wrong can be heard from responsible sources. In those cases, and in confronting issues of a very complex nature, we Presbyterians have a habit of investigating and trying to address. Most of the time such work is done at the General Assembly level, both to draw on the greatest possible resources, and also in order to speak an ethical word if possible to the widest possible audience. The Assembly is charged, among other jobs, with the responsibility "to warn or bear witness against errors in doctrine or immorality in practice in or outside the Church" (Book of Order, G–13.0103).

In previous years, Assemblies of various Presbyterian denominations have witnessed against many kinds of immorality and bad doctrine. Sometimes Assemblies have asked for the closing of fairs and expositions on Sunday, for the prohibition of liquor, for the withdrawal of armed forces from certain overseas lands, for the end of support for oppressive governments (which some Assemblies named), and for the acceptance of refugees by Americans—all complicated statements which came from careful study and prayerful consideration.

These Assembly statements sometimes influence the actions of mission programs, home missions activities, and other organizations within the Presbyterian Church. These statements can also help people in local churches in their everyday decisions and actions. Some years ago, both Assemblies that now constitute the Presbyterian Church (U.S.A.), took a stand against the methods of advertising used by a major company selling dried milk in developing nations. The actions of both Assemblies asked Presbyterians to cease buying products from that company until it changed its methods of advertising in the new nations. The actions of the Assemblies affected buying patterns for church institutions. It also helped us Presbyterians know how to address the issue.

The statements of the Assemblies brought the matter to public attention, and the company took notice. Perhaps that company will have changed its ways of doing business by the time this book is published. At any rate, many Presbyterians disagreed with the statements of the Assemblies and the actions suggested. Many Presbyterians, on the other hand, began to talk about the need to boycott products from that company temporarily. The statements could not force any Presbyterian to cease buying some items at a grocery store, nor did any statements seek to force anyone. The Assembly statements did help us at Anchorage Presbyterian, however, for we discussed the matter in Sunday school on several occasions. Several of us probably became more interested in and knowledgeable about new nations as a result of the statements. In this matter, and in many more, I am convinced Assemblies of the Presbyterian church do help us focus on caring.

7

To
Receive
Baptism

She did not cry when her parents stood in front of the congregation. Sarah Kelton, at two months old, simply looked around and took it all in. Bunnie and David, her parents, answered several questions about their own faith and their willingness to bring Sarah up in the nurture and love of God. Then we in the congregation affirmed that we would also care for her as she matures. Finally, John Ames took Sarah in his arms and baptized her. The baby seemed a bit startled as John brought her down the aisle, "I want you to meet everyone." All the while, grandparents beamed from the front pew.

About once a month we baptize infants in our particular church, about six times a year we baptize teenagers or adults. On each occasion people take vows, and we usually feel especially good as the sacrament takes place. We know baptism has been important for the church through the centuries, as has the Lord's Supper. We know Reformed teachings on it differ from some teachings of other churches, but what exactly are we doing in a baptism, and how does our understanding relate with that of other traditions?

Baptism, a Sacrament

In its practice the early church began to develop doctrine around the experiences Jesus shared with his disciples. Jesus himself had been baptized by John. He had commanded the disciples to baptize believers. From the time of Pentecost itself, apostles and disciples had baptized people. Philip even moved quickly to convert and baptize an Ethiopian, a minister in the court of the queen of the nation (Acts 8:26–40).

Special meaning came also when Peter received a dream in Joppa. He saw all kinds of animals, and he heard a voice saying, "What God has cleansed, you must not call common." Peter responded to a request from Cornelius, a centurion of the Italian Cohort, to come to Caesarea. There Peter baptized Cornelius, a Roman soldier, with all the household, when he perceived that Gentiles too had received the Holy Spirit (Acts 10).

With baptism, as with other special practices, Christians affirmed their continuity with the apostles and disciples of Jesus. In baptism, a person was initiated into the faith. In the Eastern Orthodox Churches, emphasis was put on the preparation for resurrection. In the Western, Catholic churches leaders emphasized the indelible, new character of the believer and the beginning on the sacramental path. Baptism was viewed as the first of the seven sacraments upon which the faithful depended for nourishment in grace.

Reformed leaders in the sixteenth century such as Zwingli and Calvin tried to regain a biblical perspective on faith and do away with dependence on the sacramental system, but they took different views of the meaning of baptism. Zwingli considered it almost as much trouble as it was worth. Calvin saw how important it had been in the Gospel accounts of Jesus, how Jesus had commanded disciples to baptize people, and how the Acts church had practiced it. All Reformed leaders said, however, that in the sacraments nothing magical happened in a mechanical way. Baptism could not replace faith, which came from God.

Some of those who read their Bibles felt that any *sacra-mentum*, or "sacred thing," mistook the nature of the early church practice and the demands Christ gave. These reformers argued that Zwingli, Calvin, (and Luther for that matter), went only part way in a necessary reformation. They advocated the celebration of ordinances, things Christ told people to do, but they said sacraments were wrong.

Presbyterians, since that time, have taken a middle position on the sacraments—both baptism and the Lord's Supper. We have continued to view baptism as a sacrament, but we have said sacraments in themselves do not save people or even help us to have more faith. In the words of the *Directory for the Service of God*, baptism "sets forth the grace of God in Jesus Christ and affirms that believers and their children are heirs of the covenant of grace" (*Directory for the Service of God*, S–3.02. The *Directory for the Service of God* is published as part of the *Book of Order*, prepared by the Joint Committee on Presbyterian Union. Subsequent references to the *Directory for the Service of God* refer to the edition cited.)

Infant Baptism

Presbyterians baptize the children of believers, as do Catholics, Eastern Orthodox, Anglican, Lutheran, and several other varieties of Christian communions. According to Calvin, just as infants in Israel received circumcision, so children of Christians received baptism (*Institutes* IV:14, 24). It did not bother him that the Bible records no specific baptism of children. Calvin did point to the baptism of the household of Cornelius, but he did not argue that that meant God intended for the church to baptize all infants.

We Presbyterians say that baptism of infants is a "sign and seal of God's promise to them as heirs of the covenant."

> In presenting a child for baptism parents affirm in public their duty to bring up the child to love and serve God. The congregation, too, promises to surround the child with their love and concern in Christ, that the child may continue in the community of the Church, confess Jesus Christ as Savior and Lord, and live in God's eternal kingdom.
>
> (*Directory for the Service of God*, S–3.03)

Therefore for Presbyterians the baptism of infants is a sign and seal of God's care for those particular children. It is also a promise taken by Christian parents and the wider church that the children will be educated in the faith, hopefully to receive the personal, saving knowledge of God at some future time. Presbyterians also like to quote Jesus, for on several occasions he said all must become like little children to receive the kingdom of God.

Not all Christians agree on infant baptism. Obviously, Baptists are the most outspoken critics of this practice. They point to John the Baptist, to Jesus receiving baptism as a grownup, to the baptism of early Christians such as Cornelius. They say one must first repent, then believe, and then be baptized. Other Protestant communions, such as the Disciples of Christ and the various Mennonite denominations, also practice "believer baptism." They complain that the practice of infant baptism arose in state churches, where all had to be Christian whether or not they believed.

It makes little sense to argue, since both practices have biblical bases and long traditions. Moreover, it is easy for us Presbyterians to recognize other ways of interpreting the history as valid, even if they differ from our own. When Baptist or Christian (Disciples of Christ) persons join our denomination, we have no trouble recognizing their baptism as valid. Sometimes the reverse is not the case, and we need to understand the reluctance of many to accept our baptism as valid. We should also realize that no Presbyterian parents have to submit their infants for baptism.

David and Bunnie Kelton were Presbyterians before they married. They had no hesitation presenting Sarah for baptism. On the other hand, several families at Anchorage Presbyterian have thus far not asked for their children to be baptized. The Presbyterian Church has plenty of room for them too. Whether children are baptized or not, we have a responsibility to bring them up in the knowledge and love of God.

Active Membership and Adult Baptism

At what is traditionally called "the age of discernment," children have the opportunity to make their own, personal profession of faith. Sarah Kelton, when she is about twelve years old, will be invited to join a group of children her own age and receive intensive instruction from John Ames, Mary Morgan, and several of the rest of us. She can choose to join an earlier group if she wishes, and she may refuse to go altogether to a group preparing for active membership. But in the preparation she can learn a lot about our church and about her part in it. In our congregation, that group will plan and lead Sunday worship at the end of their study as well as make their professions of faith.

Eleven years from now, Sarah Kelton may well be in a different congregation. Her father is in graduate school in mathematics and teaches, and her mother is attending business school. Chances are, in our mobile society, Sarah will profess her own faith elsewhere; and other children who were baptized elsewhere will make profession of faith in our local church. That is fine among Presbyterians. We believe that the church universal is one body of Christians on earth of which we are a little part.

Denominational mobility is another part of our modern society, as the introduction indicated. We have many people who join the Presbyterian Church in our congregation by transfer of letter and by reaffirmation of faith. People from other Reformed denominations, and those from churches that recognize the Presbyterian Church as a part of God's family receive a letter of transfer if they have been active in the previous church. Those who have not been active elsewhere, though members and baptized in the Christian faith, simply make a reaffirmation of faith. Those who have been active in another church, but in a church that does not issue letters of transfer to Presbyterian churches, also reaffirm their faith.

Today in the United States, as in times past, many people have never been baptized. When a person joins the Presbyterian Church as a teenager or as an adult, that person receives "believer baptism" among us. He or she professes personal loyalty to Jesus Christ as Lord and Savior, and the willingness to participate in the life of the church, Christ's body. Personally, I have discovered several people reluctant to join the Presbyterian Church, embarrassed that they have never been baptized. It seems no sacramental time is more joyous than the baptism of a newly professing Christian. And we Presbyterians have been rather lazy in asking folk to come to church with us, to make a profession in Jesus Christ, and to become members of Christ's body.

We can all grow in knowledge and love of God. Christian education is vitally linked with baptism, both for infants and for grownups.

Education in the Faith

Sarah Kelton will begin Sunday school very soon. At Anchorage Presbyterian Church we have a pre-school class, in which children hear Bible stories and play together with grownups. In successive classes, they learn more about the faith, taught by members of the congregation. Youth groups take trips together, and they share other activities. All these things are connected with the promises we make in baptism.

Right from the first of the Reformed tradition up to the present, Christian education has remained extremely important. The logic of its significance is very simple. If God expected each person to affirm or deny the gospel, and if saving knowledge had been given by the Holy Spirit to some people, then each person had to perceive the gospel—had to hear it. If no one could mediate the gospel, even though preachers could interpret it, and if the Bible offered everything necessary for saving knowledge, then everyone had to read the Bible. A portion of the task was the translating of the Bible into languages of the people. But another portion was in the teaching of everyone to read the Scriptures.

In places where Reformed faith flourished, literacy quickly became the rule among men (and sometimes even among women, although they had to learn in less formal settings for the most part). Other Protestant communions also emphasized education, and Catholics came to stress it for laypeople also, but none other quite as much as Reformed Christians.

When sabbath schools began more than two centuries ago, they were for the children of the poor. The poor received no education and therefore could not read the Bible for themselves. So they really had not yet heard the gospel. Presbyterians cooperated with other Protestants to bring sabbath schools to the needy as a service of evangelism and mission. Gradually, during the nineteenth century, Presbyterians came to use the sabbath schools for their own children, as well as for the poverty stricken. The same thing happened in other communions. The Sunday schools and church schools as we know them are rather recent organizations, existing from the latter part of the nineteenth century.

Presbyterian zeal for education extended to all realms. If, as we have seen, the creation is good, then knowledge of it is also good. Those in Reformed schools and colleges considered all kinds of learning important. Especially the minister should be learned in all kinds of disciplines. Thus, Harvard, Yale, Princeton, and numbers of other universities grew mainly from beginnings as Reformed seminaries where clergy and other church leaders could receive education. As the Presbyterians and Congregationalists grew apart, each group began numbers of colleges and seminaries. And the Presbyterian ministers trained in these schools opened academies in their manses across the country, where younger children could learn about God and the world.

Presbyterians cooperated in the public school movement in the nineteenth century despite the fact that they had developed a number of parochial schools. A part of their interest came from this commitment to teach each person to read. How else could each person be accountable before God? How else could Presbyterians keep their promises that children would grow in nurture and love of God?

Sunday schools, or church schools, have become a vital part of most congregations' corporate life. Some Presbyterians had already learned before the twentieth century that at different stages in growth and life people have different needs and abilities to learn about God and themselves. Today most Sunday schools have different lessons and activities for younger and older children, for those being confirmed in the church, and for adults. Some Presbyterians are also experimenting with activities that help different generations to learn from each other. The wide variety of kinds of education for the faith can offer growth for everyone.

Do Presbyterians have to go to, teach in, and support Christian education? No, there are some who do not; but at the same time, yes, it is part and parcel of the promises we make in the baptism of both infants and adults. Church schools and all the other educational opportunities are occasions for us to learn about God, ourselves, and the mission of the church.

8

To
Take
Communion

In our congregation, George James almost always bakes the bread for communion. Sometimes he bakes crusted French bread, sometimes rye bread with lots of body, sometimes individual hot cross buns. George has been an elder in the church for a number of years, and he says he just likes to prepare for the Lord's Supper by doing it. He says it gives him time to think and pray.

George knows that preparation for the Lord's Supper is extremely important in the Reformed tradition. Many Presbyterians do not make special preparation for the sacrament, though, and all of them are welcome at the table too. In fact, in recent decades most Reformed bodies have stressed the open invitation "to all baptized believers and their children" to share in the Lord's Supper. To be Presbyterian means that we do take communion, but what does it mean in our faith?

Communion, a Sacrament

Just as baptism remains a sacrament for Presbyterians, so does communion. We believe that Jesus told members of the church to celebrate it, that he promised God's special presence as communion is shared, and that Christians through the ages have continued faithfully to do it. Three words for us are synonymous: "communion," "Lord's Supper," and "eucharist" (from the Greek word for "grateful"). Jesus shared a Passover meal with his disciples. According to all the Gospels it differed a bit from the regular Jewish feast. Jesus blessed the bread and the cup after supper and he told the followers to share both (see Matt. 26:17–35; Mark 14:12–31; Luke 22:1–38; John 13:1—16:33). The eucharist is also essential in the Roman Catholic mass and in the liturgy of the Eastern Orthodox churches. Almost all kinds of Protestants celebrate communion in some fashion.

Even before the sixteenth-century Reformation and the start of a Reformed tradition, John Hus in what is now Czechoslovakia and John Wycliffe in England argued that the church should follow the Bible more closely in its teachings about communion. Martin Luther, John Calvin, and other Reformers generally agreed, but they disagreed on what happened in the celebration. This disagreement, more than any other one issue, kept Protestants from unifying in the early years of the movement.

Calvin, and the Presbyterians who follow his teaching on the Lord's Supper, have tried to steer a middle course between the "high" communion theology of Catholics and Lutherans on the one hand, and the Protestants who considered it only an act of "remembering" and "hoping" on the other. Reformed creeds have stressed that it remains a sacrament, a holy event. However, it possesses no magic, and Presbyterians are not saved by taking it.

Presbyterians understood the church as universal, the gathering of all Christians whether they believed Reformed teachings or not. It made sense for the Presbyterians to recognize God's work in all kinds of communion celebrations. While Roman Catholics sometimes considered that a Presbyterian communion service had no special power for the faithful, Presbyterians usually have not doubted God's work in the mass so long as the believers do not depend on magic there. By the same token, many times Baptists have demanded that Christians belong to a particular church in order truly to share communion, thereby expressing doubt that Presbyterian communion is a sacrament. Presbyterians have not hesitated to consider Baptist communion true, and Baptist believers are welcome at Presbyterian communion.

In communion, the bread and the wine are signs that, according to Calvin, "represent for us the invisible food that we receive from the flesh and blood of Christ." God keeps feeding us for us to grow in our commitment to Christ. We obtain both assurance and delight from the sacrament—assurance of our eternal life, and delight that God cares for us now and evermore (*Institutes* IV: 17, 1).

Serious students of the Presbyterian tradition today argue about the extent of Christ's "real presence" in the sacrament. Catholics, and many Lutherans, consider that Jesus Christ is present substantially in the sacrament itself. Presbyterians were generally thought to believe Christ was merely "represented" in the sacrament, but careful reading of Calvin's *Institutes* and other early Reformed theology shows that for many the "Spiritual Presence" they talked about was considered substantial. They wanted to guard against any mechanical understanding, but they believed that real communication of Christ's presence occurred.

Presbyterian Practice

For many generations, Presbyterians and other Calvinists "fenced the table" for the Lord's Supper. The minister or a ruling elder would go to each household during the week before a communion service. The church leader would examine all the members of the family who were full church members. Did they know important doctrine? Had they obeyed the law insofar as possible? Had they been faithful in worship and work? If members passed, they would receive tokens for communion. On the day of the service, after reading the Scripture and preaching an "Action Sermon" on the nature of the Lord's Supper, the minister would read Paul's words in 1 Corinthians 11:23–34. He would then invite all those with tokens to come forward and to sit at table. Those presenting tokens, sometimes only a small portion of the congregation, would be served communion. All the other people would either watch from outside the fenced area or else go home.

Presbyterians were paying special attention to the warning of 1 Corinthians 11:28 that if a person did not discern the body (understand what was happening), that person would incur God's judgment. Reformed churches took the Lord's Supper as primarily a "sealing ordinance," an occasion for sealing the faith of the believer in communion with God through Christ's Spirit. During the nineteenth century, Presbyterians gradually came to emphasize communion also as a "teaching ordinance," a time of learning in action of the work of Christ through the Spirit.

Typically, Presbyterians celebrated the sacrament of communion four times a year, though in some churches six times a year was also a common practice. Presbyterians would take the bread and the wine always in the context of worship. After Mr. Welch invented a process for keeping fermentation from occurring, and as the temperance movement became more powerful, over the objections of conservatives in many congregations, grape juice became the "fruit of the vine" for most Presbyterians.

Today Presbyterian churches celebrate the Lord's Supper in different ways, with varying frequency. In some places, particularly in rural areas, quarterly communion is still the habit. Many city churches take communion the first Sunday of each month. Some congregations also offer eucharistic services weekly, perhaps in a small chapel early Sunday mornings before regular worship. Youth conferences and retreats share the Lord's Supper sometimes, too. The differing customs reflect the varieties in Reformed theology today, and the impact of the ecumenical movement.

Recently, Presbyterians have begun to permit children to take communion though they are not yet active church members. In addition, many congregations have begun to celebrate Agape meals, occasions based on the meals in the early church similar to communion. A word about each of these new practices seems necessary.

Communion for Children

John Calvin had long ago said that the Lord's Supper is "by Nature incomprehensible" because it remains a mystery how Christ is united with the faithful. As Presbyterians became more interested again in his theology, and as we came in contact with other Christian traditions more fully, we moved in recent years to permit baptized children to share in the sacrament. One might say we became more modest in our claims about our own knowledge of what takes place in communion. One could also say that we began paying greater attention to some other passages in the Bible, particularly to the words of Jesus: "Let the little children come to me, and do not hinder them, for to such belongs the kingdom of heaven" (Matt. 19:14). In

addition to these reasons, another is probably that the same movement is going on in most Protestant churches that baptize children.

The *Directory for the Service of God* says that the invitation for
sharing in the Lord's Supper "shall include baptized children who
are being nurtured and instructed to participate with an understanding of the significance of the invitation to the Lord's Table and of
their response in faith" (*Directory for the Service of God*, S—3.05).
All the congregation cooperates in providing this instruction and
understanding for the children—not just the parents. At Anchorage
Presbyterian Church I notice that some children do not take communion. In fact, I notice that some adults from time to time do not
take it. I suppose the hesitation comes from the tradition, when it
was considered more a "sealing ordinance" and less a "teaching
ordinance." I think those of us who sought the changes and enjoy
the freedom of baptized children to take communion, need to understand the feelings of others with different perspectives. After all,
we acknowledge that communion offers no magical power for believers to help them in being saved. On the other hand, people
hesitant to take communion in times of feeling guilty or full of
remorse, and those who will not permit baptized children on the
road to active membership to take communion, may need to gain
understanding also.

Agape Meals and Other Celebrations

A number of Presbyterian congregations now celebrate Agape
meals from time to time. Either in conjunction with a family night
supper, or on its own, such a time can be inspirational and full of
good worship. An Agape meal, like early Christian love feasts, involves a group of Christians sharing bread and perhaps other dishes
of food as well. Sometimes the use of symbolic foods and numbers
helps remind us of certain events from the ministry of Jesus—the
use of five loaves of bread and three fish, for example. When we
gather for an Agape meal, we sing and pray. We also can learn about
one another in an informal setting.

I mention the Agape meal at this point because it is not for us a
sacrament. We Presbyterians share several kinds of celebrations that
are extremely important, full of religious meaning, but are not sac-

raments. Historically, Wednesday night prayer meetings have been a part of congregational life in many local churches. Family night suppers, too, have been special occasions for us in Anchorage and for Presbyterians in all parts of the country. Weddings and funerals are significant worship times, of special meaning to church families as to the wider congregation; and they will be discussed in chapter 11. In Memphis, Tennessee, and here in Louisville, and probably in cities across the country, Presbyterians from many congregations are gathering weekly at a central location for excellent Bible study times. These times all bear God's grace as surely as if they were sacramental in nature. Baptism and the Lord's Supper differ only in the fact that Christ promised to be present as sacraments take place.

In our Reformed tradition, especially among the Puritans, there has been a strain of faith which considered every day the Lord's Day, every Sunday an Easter. Many Presbyterians continue to share this spirit that all days are holy, all services of worship the occasion for special presence of God. Some Presbyterians from good ethical bases shy from celebrations—especially from fancy ones. Others, with varying backgrounds and with good reasons also, really enjoy the Christian seasons, the special celebrations such as Agape meals and other such events. I personally am delighted that in this area of church life we Presbyterians have many different styles and expectations. There is latitude, and Presbyterians are required only to pay special attention to the two sacraments whatever our other preferences and habits.

9

To Belong to the Church

A few years ago, Harriet Hilley, then a senior in high school, went from Anchorage Presbyterian Church to the Republic of Zaire to deliver an airplane. She and another member from the Presbyterian Church here in the United States of America represented the young people from across the church who had contributed to buy the plane. They gave it to the Protestant church in Zaire so that their evangelists and medical personnel could reach people in outlying areas of the country where roads were particularly poor. These medical and evangelistic persons could bring the gospel and serve the needs of people in other ways too, because Harriet and lots of teenagers helped.

We Presbyterians are members of a universal church. Have we heard that before? Examples of our Christian solidarity are all over the place, if we stop to notice them. Last fall, for example, I took Joong Eun Kim, his wife Gwi Yub, and their son Hyong Woo to a birthday celebration at Mt. Sterling Presbyterian Church. Dr. Kim is Professor of Old Testament at the Presbyterian seminary in Seoul, Korea, and Gwi Yub is a specialist in Christian education. In a Sunday school class, the teacher began to explore accounts in the books of Samuel about the early monarchy. Dr. Kim explained to them about the various ways in which the people of Israel viewed the king—a hope, a threat, a promise from God, a foretelling of a real messiah, and so forth. Here was a Korean teacher and minister, educated in both Korea and Switzerland, sharing with American Christians words from the Old Testament that all of us care about.

Though not so apparent all the time, our life in the Christian church universal is a real part of our being Presbyterians. Previous chapters have mentioned some formal aspects of this life. Consider, though, the belief we voice in "the communion of saints." More than a formal link with others in Presbyterian churches across the world and with all other Christians, we have a spiritual link. No wonder one of our favorite hymns is "Blessed be the tie that binds our hearts in Christian love; the fellowship of kindred minds is like to that above." No wonder the communion service with fellow Christians from across a region or nation seems particularly power-ful and moving!

As we affirm our Christianity in the Presbyterian strain of it, we are reminded of both the opportunities in our local situations and of the ways we claim responsibility in the worldwide church of Jesus Christ. In addition, we see the part corporate prayer plays in our religious life.

Member of the Whole Church

Belief and practice really do form a single fabric. In the nine-teenth and early twentieth centuries, when the missionary move-ment among Presbyterians had begun in earnest, congregations would thrill to the reports of those sent from their number to serve in other lands. I honestly think that vitality for American Christians came in large measure from the joy they shared in helping take the gospel to other lands.

One of my own favorite stories recounts the work of William Sheppard and William McCutchen Morrison in Africa. Sheppard, an early Black minister for the Presbyterian Church, U.S., and Mor-rison who graduated from the seminary I now serve, together trans-lated the gospel into the languages of several different tribal groups along the Congo River. As they evangelized, they encountered the oppression of King Leopold of Belgium, who forced exorbitant taxes from the people and whose representatives in the colonial govern-ment permitted torture of tribes that would not or could not pay. Sheppard and Morrison wrote to American and other Christians, especially to Presbyterians; and the two missionaries were sued for libel by the king. Their trial in a newly established World Court enabled the atrocities to be documented for the media. As a result the gross oppression was diminished, even as the members of the tribes learned about Jesus Christ, their Messiah.

I cannot help but believe Harriet Hilley, Sheppard, Morrison, and all the rest, in various ways, are helping Christians in America to cooperate with Christians in Central Africa. We are linked with Christians there in a special way. Personally, I take special interest in Zaire and its churches in part because other members of the wider church have been and will be drawing my interest and prayers there.

Think today of Christians in Korea, many of whom are Presbyterians. They are bringing the gospel to colleagues in ways somewhat different from our own. They emphasize small group Bible study, which might be an emphasis we Americans could better use. They also stand up when necessary to proclaim the rights of Christian people and other citizens to gather and speak freely. Some of the Christian leaders have recently spent time in jail. International bodies that thoroughly investigate reports of oppression say Christians were recently tortured there. We American Christians are linked closely with them as they evangelize and as they witness.

We American Presbyterians are linked, through the work of Christ's Spirit, to the faithful throughout the world. This identification causes us sorrow when others suffer, and we receive joy as others experience it. Naturally, we cannot know about all the other Christian communities and works of charity. Through international missions and service organizations we help others and they help us. No wonder Presbyterians have been supporters of the World Council of Churches (WCC), and Church World Service which is one of its helping organizations! No wonder we also are supporters of the World Alliance of Reformed Churches, an organization of all Presbyterian, Congregationalist, and other so-called "Calvinist" bodies!

Sometimes, when Christians in other lands have differing perspectives on needs and ways to help, American Christians have been quick to criticize such organizations. No doubt the World Council of Churches makes mistakes, just as we believe our own General Assembly is capable of error, and just as we believe we ourselves are not perfect in this life. I personally take some solace in the knowledge that the WCC, in the Church World Service work, meets the needs of starving people in Chad, Somalia, or wherever there are hungry people. I am delighted that a portion, be it ever so small, of the money I contribute to the Presbyterian Church is used by Church World Service. In fact, I feel our own family should be making greater contributions to the work.

The command of Jesus for us Christians to be "witnesses" all over the world was very clear. "You shall be my witnesses in Jerusalem and in all Judea and Samaria and to the ends of the earth" (Acts 1:8). Sometimes I think I'm in Jerusalem, sometimes in Judea, sometimes in Samaria, and sometimes in the uttermost parts of the world. Wherever I am, I know that in all these places I am to be a witness. People at Anchorage Presbyterian Church, like folks throughout America, are now traveling all over the world. Some such as John Fishbach in our congregation, will actually travel frequently to Saudi Arabia, to Israel, and to other nations in the Near East. Many others of us find ourselves in other countries for work or play or both. It seems that all of us, whether we actually travel to various countries in person, or whether our representatives are there, share in this worldwide witness—on a scale never before realized in human history.

Think of our responsibilities as Christians, both as we go to various lands and as we participate in worldwide mission and service activity! Yet all Presbyterians do not agree on ways in which we can witness. I am reminded of the time my wife and I helped a nurse in a well-baby clinic in Zaire. We served two lines of folk as mothers brought babies for malaria pills. My wife and I simply gave the mothers and infants pills. The nurse, to each mother in the other line said, "This is from the church for you, and for your baby. Go in the name of Jesus Christ." It seemed a kind of microcosm of Christian witness that day, some of us explicitly mentioning Christ and telling people about the faith while others of us witnessed by action without necessarily saying words about Jesus Christ. We Presbyterians have a history of witnessing in both ways. Certain ones of us are more inclined to one or another style of Christian witness. I really hope our belonging to the worldwide church includes both areas of witness (and many more), as we travel for work and play in various countries and as we participate with those who share missions here and abroad.

Member of the Local Church

Our Christian community is not just worldwide. It is also very near at hand. We take care lest we act like a character in one of George Bernard Shaw's plays who went forever to meetings in behalf of people on the other side of the globe while that person's family fell to pieces. Our own family and our church families deserve attention, as we consider what it means to be a Presbyterian. As we have seen from the illustrations within Anchorage Presbyterian, many of us have different interests and gifts. Elsie Robinson, who spoke profoundly about trust in God, says she is reluctant to speak in public, yet she is a real help to me and no doubt to lots of other members. Wayne Perkey, who leads our Issues Class, is not at all hesitant to speak in public. John Fishbach, who represents Jesus Christ in many nations and among many peoples, is not able to be a regular member of a committee. Each of us has different skills. Lan Arendson and Herb Bell are good in financial matters, as are Ruth Ann Boklage and David Haney. Kay Von Deylen has taken a great deal of responsibility in helping the Laotian refugee families we sponsored. And Jamie Meyer may be "just a high school student," but he has the best reading voice (and bass in the choir) of any of us. The women's organization does things others of us cannot do. So does the leadership of the "Readings for the Handicapped." Yet all of us together form a congregation.

We Presbyterians belong to the church universal in local congregations. In addition to the beliefs we share about this fact (discussed in chapter 4), we share also a mutual dependence. Sometimes I personally am emotionally moved by the sense that we all cooperate to be together what none of us could be individually. When a member of the congregation needs help, people pitch in and help. It may not be the same people every time, for different ones of us are closer to some families and individuals than to others. There seem to be some "all purpose players" on our congregational team, such as

Loetta Hopkins and Nancy Durham, who are willing to single out people not being cared for; and they go and care for those folks.

Now, again as at every point, we Presbyterians remember that churches contain sinful people, even as we serve God and God's creation. At Anchorage, as in every congregation, many folk do not seem to bear their share of the load. Many others could do more than we do. "None of us is righteous, save Christ our Lord." Though Presbyterians are not forced to do a certain amount of work in a local church, the needs of that congregation and a member's own gifts quickly become apparent. It seems a direct responsibility of Presbyterians to share in the life of a congregation even as we share in the worldwide church.

Time, Talents, Money

A traditional way we Presbyterians have expressed responsibility has been in terms of time, talents, and money. As we recognize all life, faith, love, and other gifts come from God, so we recognize our responsibility to render back a portion of what has been given us in these areas.

Reformed Christians have remembered that the tithe was extremely important in the life of the people of Israel. Though Jesus lived, died, and rose fulfilling a law we could not fulfill, we see the giving back to God of one tenth of God's gifts to us as a good starting point for Christian living. Presbyterians in other generations and in other cultures today use the tithe as a natural yardstick.

Others point to differing needs of people during different stages of living, and argue that a more flexible measure is better. A person could leave a portion of an estate for the work of the church, for example. In whatever way we can, Presbyterians need to share in the work of the church with the giving (or rendering back) of significant portions of our money.

Perhaps the giving of time and talents is even more important. Almost every congregation possesses many people of immense talent and skill. Think of what the local church could be if each gave according to skill and interest, both to the local church and to the universal church. Presbyterian churches in other lands may be looking right now, as many usually are, for a man or woman willing to be a printer, a farmer, a business consultant, an architect, a medical technician, a teacher, a nurse, or a minister for a period of time. A man, woman, couple, or family can serve another Christian body or an ecumenical ministry for a particular period of time today. Some churches want that kind of service especially. Again, our congregation and every other I know would love to have more help from members skilled in particular areas of ministry. To be a Presbyterian is to consider with the church what areas of talents and what commitments of time can be used for the needs of the work of the church.

Prayer

Our prayer life is another part of belonging to the church, as it is a part of corporate worship. Our spiritual links with other Christians in our locale and across the earth are shared in our prayers. As Presbyterians, we have a tradition of praying together, but we let no priest or minister do all our praying for us. Corporate prayer is supplemented with private prayer.

Jesus had many things to say about prayer, such as the fact that we should be modest in our words and phrases (Matt. 6:5–6). He also gave an example of prayer, which we Protestants follow in different fashion from the way Catholics do. But to explore the possibilities of prayer would take another book, and we need to consider quickly other things more mundane in our Presbyterian commitment—citizenship, for example.

10

To
Obey
the Law

"Yes, we are working rather hard on the sewer lines." Peyton Hoge, the mayor of Anchorage was talking to our Issues Class in Sunday school. He is a member of the church, and periodically he is invited to talk with us about the major community issues, the proposal to reorganize county government, and other political matters. Many of the members of the congregation live in the little city of Anchorage, but even those of us who do not reside in the community itself see the importance of his presence with us. Do the police need a pay increase? Is the bridge unsafe across one of the town's creeks? What issues will face the state during the coming year? Peyton is knowledgeable about all these things.

Peyton Hoge is not the only politician who talks with us in the church. From time to time our local state representative comes to a church dinner, or the candidates for political office are invited to debate for a church forum. Most of us see responsible citizenship in the nation and community as a part of our Christian commitment. Very frequently sparks will fly when some of us argue for better schools, while others of us seek no new taxes. Again, we are not all agreed about food stamps, aid for college students, the welfare structure, criteria for election of officials, or other significant areas of political decision making. Yet we are willing to listen to knowledgeable people describe their points of view.

I would venture to say all of us at Anchorage Presbyterian Church want to obey the law. More than that, we seek to belong to a civil society as mature and active citizens. What is it about the Reformed faith that fosters such commitment? Is it a different stance from that of other Christian bodies in America?

Render to Caesar

Historically, Christians have been "good citizens" in most lands since the time of Constantine. Jesus, frequently quoted on the subject, said "Render therefore to Caesar the things that are Caesar's, and to God the things that are God's" (Matt. 22:21). He spoke about the paying of a colonial ruler in the coins that the colonial government minted. Since early in the fourth century, Christians in the West have been the favored people of the state almost all the time. When barbarians overthrew Rome, they may have destroyed a part of the civilization but they were as much Christian as the people they overthrew had been. When the Reformation occurred, various parties may have called each other "pagans," but in fact Protestants of various kinds were struggling with Catholics—all at least nominally Christian.

Reformed leaders in Switzerland, France, areas of what is now Germany, England, Scotland, the Netherlands, and elsewhere wanted their faith the established faith of the realm. Even in American colonies, Puritans zealously guarded the "city set on a hill," the favored status of Calvinism in several New England colonies. When early Presbyterians came to America from Scotland and Northern Ireland, they expected to obtain favored status for their faith in the new world.

Since the Revolutionary War and the forming of voluntary religious denominations—Protestant, Catholic, Jewish, and others—the United States has experimented with a new pattern of church-state relationships. We Presbyterians today in the United States are heirs of all this history, and it has a bearing on our thought about politics as on social responsibility. Many scholars argue our Calvinism has an effect on our sense of economics also.

Since at least the fifth century, we Christians have perceived ourselves belonging to two "cities," mutually dependent yet not identical. One city is the city of "human beings," in which nothing is perfect. Yet in the human city, life can be more just sometimes than others. The other city is the city of God, in which we belong but do not yet live. So the realm of "Caesar" has been interpreted as something in which we have citizenship, quite different from the situation in which Jesus and the disciples spoke about politics. The "realm of God" has its beginning in the church universal, though the believers on earth are not the same thing as the "communion of saints" in heaven.

In America, where Thomas Jefferson coined the phrase, "a wall of separation" has partially existed between church and state, and the realms have sometimes been seen as mutually exclusive. Occasionally even Presbyterians have seen the spiritual as unrelated to the political, especially as the doctrine of the "spirituality of the church" developed in the south. That phrase came to be used widely in the late nineteenth century. Some Presbyterians have gone even further, arguing as Mennonites and some Baptists that Christians should shun the world, which is a "veil of tears." A few have refused to vote in political elections because America did not recognize Jesus Christ as Lord of the land.

For the most part, however, Presbyterians have been vitally involved in the duties of citizenship. Most joined the ranks of the revolutionaries at the time of independence (though some good Presbyterians sided with Great Britain and even fought in behalf of America remaining a colony). A Presbyterian, John Witherspoon, was the only member of the clergy to sign the Declaration of Independence. A member of the British Parliament wrote home during the war to say it was a "Presbyterian rebellion." After the formation of the United States, Presbyterians have served in almost every elective office in the land. Several presidents, including Woodrow Wilson, have been active Presbyterians. Numerous members of the Supreme Court, members of Congress far out of proportion to denominational numbers, and scores of governors have been Presbyterians.

Presbyterians by and large have viewed the civil government as a separate realm from the church. However, we have generally seen the law as a good influence on civil life. We have considered that governments should protect the freedom of persons to gather in expression of religious beliefs. We have considered that churches should not control governments either. Rather, because all institutions keep a degree of human sinfulness, systems of checks and balances both within the church, within the state, and between church and state are healthy.

In earlier decades Roman Catholics did not usually support such a position on church and state, coming frequently to America from nations in which a state church had existed. When American Catholics did speak up for religious freedom they sometimes received rebukes from Rome. More recently, Catholics have become quite open in thinking about the legitimate independence of church and state. Lutherans, Methodists, and Episcopalians have also shared similar positions to that of the Presbyterians. Some Baptists, especially members of the more closed associations, seem to think the church should dominate political affairs. American Baptist Convention members, most Southern Baptists, and almost all National Baptists, stand in the tradition of desiring separation of church and state, some more forcefully than Presbyterians.

Third Use of the Law

Reformed church people have shared a particular viewpoint on the usefulness of the law for Christians and for all society. John Calvin, whose interpretation on the uses of the law differed from views of other Reformers, said that God gave law for three reasons: (1) to bring the elect to salvation into repentance, by the work of the Holy Spirit; (2) to restrain those who seek to do evil and care little or nothing for justice or mercy; and, (3) to teach the godly "the nature of the Lord's will" (*Institutes* II: 7, 12).

Martin Luther, leaders in the Anabaptist or radical wing of reform, and most others who came to be Protestants outside the camp of Calvin, merely contrasted law and gospel. God gave the law, which the people of Israel and everyone else broke. Then God gave Jesus Christ to save those who depended on him rather than in their ability to keep the law. Luther set law against gospel. Calvin said law continues to function positively for believers, as a teacher for us all. This emphasis on the "third use of the law" traditionally distinguishes Presbyterians and other Reformed Christians from the rest of Protestantism.

Calvin followed the teachings of the Apostle Paul in emphasizing the "third use" of the law, as Luther followed Paul in contrasting law and gospel. In Galatians, to name just one example of Calvin's use of the Bible, Paul said, "For the whole law is fulfilled in one word, 'You shall love your neighbor as yourself.' But if you bite and devour one another take heed that you are not consumed by one another" (Gal. 5:13–15). Again, Paul said a bit later, "Bear one another's burdens and so fulfill the law of Christ" (Gal. 6:2). Calvin also followed the statement of Jesus that he had come to fulfill the law rather than to abolish it.

No wonder, then, John Calvin and others after him in our tradition have paid so much attention to the Ten Commandments. The classic confessions of the Reformed churches, such as the *Heidelberg Catechism*, the *Westminster Confession*, and the *Larger and Shorter Catechisms*, spell out each of the commandments, and the *Westminster Standards* say what each means in part. Early Reformed congregations in each Lord's Day service took the time to recite all the commandments. After all, when that rich young man had asked Jesus about being saved what had Jesus replied first? Being a Christian among early Presbyterians meant being delivered from dependence on the law for salvation. The work of the Holy Spirit in the life of believers enabled followers to come closer to obedience.

Presbyterians, and most other Protestants, divide the Ten Commandments in tablets of four and six, the first four dealing with obedience to God, and the second six dealing with love of neighbor. Catholics, in contrast, divide them in tablets of five and five, including obedience to fathers and mothers among those dealing with God. Almost all Christians have understood that the moral law remains for people after the coming of Jesus Christ; only the ceremonial law no longer applied in the new time.

This attention to the law as a teacher for the righteous and for the redeemed naturally related to certain civil laws for Presbyterians. Reformed Christians, for example, heard the commandment to "Remember the sabbath day, to keep it holy" (Exod. 20:8). In the sixteenth century, Reformed Christians began to punish "sabbath-breakers" with some harshness. That idea of a Puritan sabbath, in which the civil government made rules about keeping "the Lord's Day," has been very important in America also. Even today most states forbid the sale of alcohol on Sundays during certain hours, and many local governments have more thorough rules about activity on Sundays. All these "blue laws," more important just a few years ago than they are today, came from a sense of the power of the moral law in society. Scholars today are studying the impact of the "Calvinist worldview" in forming American character. Some say no other idea has been more significant than this worldview, though most people today do not recognize its source.

Higher Law

As almost all other religious people, Presbyterians recognize that human law has limitations. Even if well-designed and well-enforced, human law will not keep perfect justice. Nor can it inject mercy into the social system. Frequently, human laws are less than well-designed and they are enforced unfairly. Christians recognize that God's law transcends human law. Presbyterians are more willing than most Christians to obey "higher law," given our beliefs about the sinfulness of all people and the duty of the faith.

Paul spoke of the "higher law" as the law of love, "a still more excellent way" (1 Cor. 12:31). He had been willing to suffer imprisonment for his mission work, which went against the law as interpreted by local magistrates. Indeed, the whole Christian tradition is full of people standing for higher law against oppressive human laws, just as the tradition is full of Christians protesting against their colleagues who claimed "higher law" as a basis of action.

Note that every Christian working in behalf of revolution, including Presbyterians fighting for an independent United States of America, claims allegiance to "the higher law of God." Over the years different issues have become part of the Presbyterian claim for the authority of "higher law." During the struggle for Prohibition, teetotal Presbyterians sometimes shut down taverns illegally in the name of higher law. During the civil rights struggle some Presbyterians disobeyed laws enforcing segregation. Today many Presbyterians invoke "higher law" in withholding taxes meant to support nuclear weapons development. In each case, other Presbyterians have objected that these people were "disobedient."

While from our Reformed tradition we can see clearly our responsibility to obey the law, we see also the tradition of civil disobedience as a part of that duty sometimes. Perceiving the nature of obedience is not simple for Presbyterians, nor for any Christians who understand our dual citizenship—in the city of God and the human city. Frequently we Presbyterians of different attitudes and varying backgrounds have been intolerant of one another. Some of us chafe at the impatience of others. Others of us feel the call of particular visions of justice and mercy. Can there be room, as much as possible, for our differences as we seek to obey the law? All Presbyterians recognize that none of us possesses perfect righteousness. We all "see through a glass darkly" as we try to be obedient.

11

To Anticipate the Kingdom

The memorial service for Helen Sherrill was a special occasion. We gathered, young and old, led by John Ames and a former minister of Anchorage Presbyterian Church to give thanks for her life and to share remembrance of her with members of her family. Mrs. Sherrill had been a member of Anchorage Presbyterian for several decades, and her husband had attended faithfully with her for years before his death. She was a specialist in early childhood development, and she had given untold energy to the efforts of the congregation in Christian education. She had been a tireless worker in behalf of the Bellewood Home for Children, too. When women were eligible for ordination as ruling elders, she became one of the first. Mostly, though, she was a faithful Christian person, rearing children in love and nurture, caring for those in need, and greeting strangers warmly. When we first visited Anchorage Church, she welcomed us warmly.

Helen Sherrill lived in anticipation of the kingdom of God, to which she already hoped to belong while she served among us. When she died, we felt keenly her loss from among us. Why, even in the nursing home she had retained good humor and sought to help those around her! Of course we would miss her! However, we knew in the assurance of our faith granted by the Holy Spirit, that Helen Sherrill had joined fully the kingdom to which she already belonged. Our service of worship was a "Witness to the Resurrection." We joined her children, other family, and longtime friends in affirming the power of Christ's resurrection, Helen's, and our own.

In our affirmation of the authority of the Bible, and in our following the confessions of Reformed Christian's communities, we Presbyterians believe God will care for us after death as God has provided for us through life. Jesus Christ said many things about the nature of eternal life, and the creeds of the church have mentioned resurrection also. Assurance of salvation, according to John Calvin, was one of the benefits of Christ in our behalf. God's predestination of the elect was another. All these beliefs together seek to describe our glimpses into the reality beyond earthly, human life. All are important for the Presbyterian.

Eternal Life in the Bible

"The Lord is my shepherd, I shall not want. . . . Even though I walk through the valley of the shadow of death, I fear no evil; for thou art with me" (Ps. 23:1, 4). Long before the coming of Jesus, the people of Israel considered God's providence eternal. Psalms from different periods in Israel's history attest to the continuity in their faith.

Jesus did teach more about eternal life, and he specifically told disciples he would provide it for them. "Truly, truly, I say to you, he who believes has eternal life" (John 6:47). Again, Jesus said to Martha, "I am the resurrection and the life; he who believes in me, though he die, yet shall he live" (John 11:25). The narratives in which each of these sayings occurs tell about life eternal, and resurrection as a part of it.

Jesus also spoke frequently about the "kingdom of heaven." Many of the parables tell about what the kingdom is like—a sower of good seeds who separates wheat from tares after an enemy sowed weed seeds in the crop (Matt. 13:24–30), a grain of mustard seed (Matt. 13:31–32), leaven in bread (Matt. 13:33), and a merchant of fine pearls finding one worth everything (Matt. 13:45–46). The kingdom of heaven, as Jesus described it, was not altogether otherworldly. He said it began in the hearts of people, and life on earth had much to do with it. On the other hand, the kingdom of heaven was not just a part of this world. It had to do with eternity, with life everlasting, and with resurrection.

Jesus addressed his disciples with a promise: "Let not your hearts be troubled; believe in God, believe also in me. In my father's house are many rooms; if it were not so, would I have told you that I go to prepare a place for you? And when I go and prepare a place for you, I will come again and will take you to myself, that where I am you may be also" (John 14:1–3).

The early church heard the promise, and some thought Jesus would return within their lifetimes to bring in his kingdom of heaven. It gave many pause when believers died. Paul wrote several of his epistles at least in part to meet this situation. To the Corinthians, for example, Paul said the gospel depended on the resurrection of Jesus. "For I delivered to you as of first importance what I also received, that Christ died for our sins in accordance with the scriptures, that he was buried, that he was raised on the third day in accordance with the scriptures" (1 Cor. 15:3–4). If Christ had arisen, Paul argued, how could people claim there was no resurrection? If Christ had not been raised, then the gospel was false at its core. "But in fact Christ has been raised from the dead, the first fruits of those who have fallen asleep" (1 Cor. 15:20).

Sometimes the Bible tells a little about the nature of eternal life. There would be no giving and taking in marriage, Jesus told one person who was trying to trick him (Mark 12:25). There would be a judgment, according to many writers portraying the sayings of Jesus. Life would be quite different. Apocalyptic books, such as the book of Revelation, give a gorgeous picture:

> Then I saw a new heaven and a new earth; for the first heaven and the first earth had passed away, and the sea was no more. And I saw the holy city, new Jerusalem, coming down out of heaven from God, prepared as a bride adorned for her husband . . . and God himself will be with them; he will wipe away every tear from their eyes, and death shall be no more, neither shall there be mourning nor crying nor pain any more.
>
> (Revelation 21:1–4)

The book of Revelation, as other apocalyptic books, speaks in symbols more vague than those in other parts of the Bible. It speaks of a heaven with pearl gates and gold streets, of choruses of angels, and of the fall of cosmic evil. But all language is symbolic to some degree, and Reformed readers of the Bible have usually been hesitant to say too much about the nature of resurrection, eternal life, or the rest of the results of salvation. Indeed, most Christians have remained modest about such matters, and with good reason.

The Resurrection of the Dead

In one of its earliest creeds, the Nicene Creed, the church said simply that Jesus "rose again according to the Scriptures, and ascended into heaven, and sitteth on the right hand of the Father." Jesus "shall come again with glory to judge both the quick and the dead, whose kingdom shall have no end." The Nicene Creed concluded with another simple sentence: "And we look for the resurrection of the dead, and the life of the world to come." Subsequent creeds have not added much by way of spelling out the nature of resurrection or life in the kingdom of heaven.

From its very beginning, Christianity moved into a society in which Greek ideas dominated thought and Greek language shared with Latin the center stage for communication. As in the case of church debates about the nature of Jesus Christ as divine and human, so in the case of life after death, different cultures used various expressions to describe it. Greek thought generally focused on immortality of the soul. Such eternal life had been taught by philosophers centuries before the coming of Christian missionaries. Soon, and for most of Christian history, the resurrection of the body and the immortality of the soul were seen as the same thing.

Recently, with language study and with modern philosophy, many have contrasted the two expressions. They say Christianity teaches resurrection of the body, not immortality of the soul. Personally, I can see little difference in the expressions, although perhaps resurrection of the body does give a bit more of a sense that the whole person is involved in life eternal. Presbyterians undoubtedly use many varying expressions, including "pass over Jordan," "be with God," and "see face to face." All these, and many others, are fine biblical metaphors to talk about a life to come. I am delighted our communion does not become preoccupied with speculation about the nature of eternal life, and such an attitude seems to be in harmony with John Calvin's.

Calvin used the image of God talking in a kind of baby talk to us, not just in matters about resurrection but in the whole Bible. The varieties of images in the Bible, said Calvin, did not prove God changed. Rather it showed God's accommodation to our limited capacity for knowledge and faith (*Institutes* II:11, 13). In other words, when the people considered the world flat, with heaven above them, God's accommodation involved the use of images which told divine truth in that worldview. Our worldview of a solar system in a galaxy among other such clusters of spheres means that God's truth comes to us in language we can fathom, too. All the same, Presbyterians have many differing conceptions of the nature of eternal life, resurrection, and even of salvation. We can hold them well without necessarily inflicting them on all the rest of us. Our modesty in this area of doctrine becomes our situation as a small portion of a human population on one of the medium planets in a rather small solar system. We can affirm the teachings of the Bible and the tradition in which we are sharing all the same.

Predestination

Though Presbyterians today do not brag about "our doctrine" anywhere I have been, it still seems necessary with the mention of Calvin, eternal life, and the Bible's teachings to say something about predestination. After all, that is the first of Presbyterian idiosyncracies, is it not?

The first thing about predestination is that it did not originate with John Calvin, the *Westminster Confession*, or sesquipedalian ministers. It comes from the Bible. Paul, in the very middle of the epistle to the Romans, says that we know "in everything God works for good with those who love him, who are called according to his purpose." Then Paul goes on to use the word: "For those whom (God) foreknew he also predestined to be conformed to the image of his Son. . . . And those whom he predestined he also called; and those whom he called he also justified; and those whom he justified he also glorified" (Rom. 8:28–30). Again, in the epistle to the Ephesians Paul said God had blessed us, "even as he chose us in him before the foundation of the world, that we should be holy and blameless before him" (Eph. 1:4). Paul did not think he was saying anything unusual either, for he and the rest of the early Christians believed they had been predestined to follow Jesus Christ. Moreover, through the history of the church until the eighteenth century at least, few if any leaders had failed to mention this important doctrine, much less openly deny it. St. Thomas Aquinas, who influenced Catholic theology perhaps more than anyone else, said almost everything Calvin did about predestination. Thus, it was not innovation among Reformed Christians.

Second, it was considered by Calvin just one of the "benefits of Jesus Christ for us," alongside prayer, resurrection, and several other things. Calvin recognized the trap in dwelling on predestination, but he said he felt compelled to follow the Bible. What Calvin evidently took for a word of comfort, a solace when things were particularly difficult, some Reformed thinkers after him emphasized a lot. Calvin spoke more modestly about predestination than did his successors. He said Jesus had talked about sheep and goats at the last judgment, and so, God must know those saved from before all time and those condemned. What God knew remained God's business, he said; we should treat everyone as members of the elect to salvation.

Third, however, Reformed thinkers did pride themselves on the doctrine and sometimes they said "predestination showed" in people. This seems to me exactly opposite of the point Jesus made about sheep and goats, when both groups of people seem surprised! At any rate, they did say people could sometimes judge whether a person was predestined to glory or to destruction by observing God's care for that person on earth. Some passages from the Psalms, for example, supported such a claim. At any rate, these theologians blew the doctrine of predestination out of proportion and said that belief in the doctrine was essential among themselves. They also pictured God the impassive judge, a harsh portrait that invited John Wesley's rebuttal. Wesley, who started the Methodist movement in England and America, said first of all, God is love. He emphasized the Bible's teachings about prevenient grace, about Christian freedom, and about God caring in mercy. Presbyterians frequently contrasted themselves with the Arminians, who said God depended more on love than on eternal decrees in working providence.

In the early twentieth century, two major Presbyterian bodies in the United States, the United Presbyterian Church, U.S.A. and the Presbyterian Church, U.S. took steps to make sure the doctrine was not overstated. They changed the standards under which they existed in order to speak of God's mercy and love. Presbyterians today can affirm Christian freedom, a compassionate God, and sound for all the world like Methodists if we wish.

We Presbyterians properly have kept reading the whole Bible. Our doctrines and our lifestyles are supposed to reflect that fact. And some of the teachings of Jesus, some of the law and prophets, letters and other writings in the Bible do proclaim things difficult to hear. We therefore have a good reputation among Christians as people willing still to hear the "hard doctrines," those about human sinfulness, divine judgment, and God's might to accomplish that judgment. A part of our source in this continuing effort to hear the "whole gospel" comes from attention to predestination.

These topics easily become more complicated. I discovered this fact anew as I tried recently to describe Calvinism, Arminianism, and the rest in encyclopedia articles. Interested Presbyterians can turn to some of the good resources named in the section "For Further Study" to continue learning about our understandings of resurrection, predestination, and the like. We need now to look one more time at the whole fabric of the faith together.

12

To
Grow
in Grace

Again, Sunday morning dawns. We find ourselves in the pew behind the Hilleys, parents of Harriet, and also of John who is a senior in college. Behind us sit the Jameses. Mrs. Elliott is there, and so are most of the rest of the folk I have been talking about. Our associate pastor, Mary Morgan, rises to read the Gospel and to preach. She reads from the Gospel, and then she reminds us of our tasks with the younger generations. "If our children come to church and hear one thing taught in Sunday school but see the institution functioning in a very different way," she warns, "chances are they will view Christianity as an outworn ideal."

On the brighter side, she declares that she values attempts made by people in Anchorage Presbyterian Church to integrate Christian faith and life. Will we concentrate on real Christian education? She challenges us, "With God's Spirit at work, a new generation may one day leave us to serve Christ."

We congregate also in the parking lot after the worship, exchanging news and asking about family. We also congregate on a hayride, in a stewardship lunch meeting, in a funeral parlor, in a committee meeting. Our particular church in many ways seeks to learn and do the will of God. Our church building may have termites, our old organ may be off-key, and our witness may not be up to snuff either. Still, we are a Presbyterian church going about its business. Our session represents us as a church court, and their representatives are our representatives also in presbytery, along with John and Mary, our ministers. Through our benevolent gifts, we are tied to Presbyterians and other Christians throughout the world—people who seek to bring the gospel to all nations. Through our prayers and acts of caring, we are tied to lots of other people and to the whole of God's creation.

It is not easy to keep a big picture of the faith, to see a part of our church struggling to feed hungry people in Ethiopia, to see a minister in Lesotho baptizing new Christians and be a part of the pledge we will help nurture the converts, to see Christians teaching in Japan, to see British Christians building a television ministry. It is not easy to give up luxuries ourselves so that others of God's children can have necessities for life. Nor is it a simple thing to try to follow Jesus in daily work, rearing children, or expecting God's kingdom to come on earth as in heaven. Yet we Christians of the Presbyterian family seek to do just those things. We aim to grow in grace, to worship God fully, and to "walk the walk while we talk the talk."

Sanctification

Objective observers of Reformed Christians who have not experienced the faith frequently comment on what they call an "irony" about us. How is it that Presbyterians and other Reformed Christians claim to believe in predestination, divine providence, the Holy Spirit giving all good things, and the failure of good works to help in salvation? Yet, at the same time Reformed Christians have been and remain among the most intense workers in proclaiming the gospel and doing good deeds. How can the two things both be true?

We Presbyterians can answer quickly that we are just doing our duty. The Reformed faith has no room for a "perfect Christian" in this life as does the Holiness movement. Nevertheless, we should work fervently in behalf of God's law and Christ's command. Jesus said, "If you love me, you will keep my commandments" (John 14:15). Can any Christian do less? By the same token, we affirm the "communion of saints" as firmly as Catholics, though we do not think anyone except Jesus can be a mediator between ourselves and God. No one has a surplus of merit except Jesus.

Presbyterians have called the belief in God's Spirit enabling our good work "sanctification." *The Larger Catechism*, in one classic statement of doctrine, says:

> Sanctification is a work of God's grace, whereby they,
> whom God hath, before the foundation of the world, chosen
> to be holy, are, in time, through the powerful operation of
> his Spirit, applying the death and resurrection of Christ unto
> them, renewed in their whole man after the image of God;
> having the seeds of repentance unto life, and all other saving
> graces, put into their hearts, and those graces so stirred up,
> increased and strengthened, as that they more and more die
> unto sin, and rise into newness of life.
>
> (*Westminster Larger Catechism*, A.75)

There you have it—a compact statement of the meaning of sanctification, which is related to predestination, justification, and the power of the Spirit. Sanctification is the process by which we Christians do integrate faith and work, but our fabric of living comes increasingly from God's Spirit.

What does sanctification mean? It means we grow in grace. Gradually as we practice the discipline and faith, we are enabled to be better Christians. This is the kind of Christian life Paul prayed the Colossians would be able to live. He asked "that you may be filled with the knowledge of [God's] will in all spiritual wisdom and understanding, to lead a life worthy of the Lord, fully pleasing to him, bearing fruit in every good work and increasing in the knowledge of God" (Col. 1:9–10). Sanctification means that we "put on the Lord Jesus Christ" (Rom. 13:14). Sanctification means that "our light shines," as chapter 4 described. But the purpose of it all, according to Reformed faith, is not to make us good or perfect. The point or purpose is to praise God, to render back in as good a life as possible the gifts of the Spirit, the new life in Christ, which has been given to us.

Piety

Among Presbyterians, the word is seldom used anymore, but that word "piety" describes well the attitude of Reformed faith. It means "reverence" and "devotion" to God. Historically, Presbyterians have sought to make all of life an act of piety. Perhaps we do well to remember some of the elements of this traditional lifestyle. Our own tasks today may differ, and our worship styles may not be the same but we can learn from recalling the piety of other times.

In Presbyterian homes a hundred years ago, for example, the whole family would gather nightly for Bible reading and prayer. Some families are able still to engage in such a special time of devotion daily, and others of us do it when complex schedules allow. The saying of "blessings" regularly at meals and the reading of verses from the Bible are a part of this tradition, all acts of piety, but also a part of Presbyterian piety historically has been the commitment of an entire family to help people or groups in need. Another part was the regular discussion of theology or values, so that younger Christians might learn "why" mature Christians did (or refrained from) certain activities.

At the turn of the century, Presbyterian denominations tried to make every family of members engage in family devotions. The institution of a "Family Altar" program, in which folk had to report their piety, may have served to kill the vitality of it for many. As in many other things, Presbyterian piety has differed among individuals, congregations, and denominations. Many Presbyterians do not live in nuclear families, and piety takes a variety of forms according to needs and opportunities. Notice, though, that such acts of devotion merely focus deeper, more profound reverence and devotion.

Many other aspects of Christian living for Presbyterians become acts of piety, not just the obvious things such as family devotions, personal devotions, refraining from commerce on Sunday when permitted, attending worship regularly, and "being constant in prayer." I recall the piety of a carpenter who said he did the best job possible as an act of praise. At Anchorage Presbyterian Church, when the young people gathered on a Saturday to help an elderly woman clean her yard, it was an act of piety. When Nancy Durham, Mary Bell, or others of the drivers for Meals on Wheels take hot food to poor, shut-in people, they are performing acts of devotion. When a business person seeks to be fair to all customers, there is piety. When a physician from our congregation stays with a member who is ill for a conversation to allay anxiety, there is reverence for God in human kindness. All of these actions, in the one fabric of living to praise God, make sense together.

Piety is not just action, though. It also involves the inner life of the Christian. Piety is the love for God shared with a love for other people and for the whole creation. The grace of Christ, which enables prayer and devotion, forms the spiritual expression appropriate for the individual. Presbyterian piety in this realm is almost impossible to discuss, yet it has formed a significant part of being a Presbyterian and it still does.

One way to mention the distinctive nature of Reformed piety is to use the words of the Psalms. In seeking to depend upon the Bible's authority, Presbyterians have relied on the Psalms as special expressions of devotion useful for piety. So in the discipline, as a Presbyterian engaged in seeking to praise God, sometimes a gorgeous day will suggest "The heavens are telling the glory of God; and the firmament proclaims his handiwork" (Ps. 19:1). When times are tough, the Presbyterian will "lift up my eyes to the hills, from whence does my help come? My help comes from the LORD who made heaven and earth. He will not let your foot be moved" (Ps. 121:1–3). The worship service will remind the Presbyterian to "Make a joyful noise to the LORD, all the lands!" (Ps. 100:1). The meeting of a good friend will render "Bless the LORD, O my soul; and all that is within me" (Ps. 103:1). At an occasion for cheating or saying something untrue comes "O LORD, thou hast searched me and known me! Thou knowest when I sit down and when I rise up; thou discernest my thoughts from afar" (Ps. 139:1–2). Gradually, imperceptibly, the Christian moves into a "living in the Psalms" as a portion of piety. Notice that the discipline of learning the Psalms is involved, that a discerning from among them the ones that meet occasions will take practice. Notice also how poorly such a way of piety is expressed in this effort, but there is one, typical way in which Presbyterian piety has been lived.

I guess the fear today is that we Presbyterians in exercising piety might be substituting little ways of praying and thinking for real, substantial living. What would we call the hollow saying of little prayers, or the emphasis on formal parts of praise? "Piosity?" Jesus said, "When you pray, go into your room and shut the door and pray to your Father who is in secret" (Matt. 6:6). Presbyterian piety at its worst has sometimes made a show of righteous living and fancy praying. At its best Presbyterian and Reformed piety has been quite full of real substance. It has been a way of life; and though aspects of it may differ among us with our many various needs and gifts, it can be a way of life for us today, too.

For Further Study

This book has offered just a brief introduction to the Presbyterian Church. I hope you will want to read and think a lot about the Christian faith and about our experience as Presbyterians within it. Here are a few of the many books which can offer next steps in learning about ourselves, our history, and our witness.

John Leith, *An Introduction to the Reformed Faith: A Way of Being the Christian Community* (Atlanta: John Knox, 1977) tells in an accurate and interesting way the history of the Presbyterians and many of the beliefs we share.

Lefferts Loetscher, *A Brief History of the Presbyterians* (Philadelphia: Westminster, 1978) offers another, chronological history of the Reformed churches, especially here in the United States.

Felix Gear, *Our Presbyterian Belief* (Atlanta: John Knox, 1980) speaks about basic doctrine in a rather simple way.

Walter Lingle and John Kuykendall, *Presbyterians, Their History and Beliefs* (Atlanta: John Knox, 1978) is particularly good as a study book for looking at both theology and history in groups and church school classes.

Dewey Wallace, *Puritans and Predestination: Grace in English Protestant Theology* (Chapel Hill: University of North Carolina Press, 1982) may be very heavy reading, but it treats that strain of predestination thought better than any other studies I have read.

John T. McNeill, *The History and Character of Calvinism* (New York: Oxford, 1954) remains for me the best book overall for teaching about Presbyterians (and our cousins) throughout the world.

Now I need to follow my own advice and recommend finally, thorough knowledge of three books: *The Holy Bible*; *The Constitution of the Presbyterian Church (U.S.A.)* which includes Part I: Book Of Confessions and Part II: Book of Order; and John Calvin, *Institutes of the Christian Religion* (Philadelphia: Westminster, 1960), the best edition.